Memos for Mystics

Other Writings by Elsa Joy Bailey

The Uncommon Book of Prayer

The Uncommon Book of Christmas

Questions: A Few Simple Inquiries into Reality

These books are available through the website:
www.elsajoy.com

Memos for Mystics

Elsa Joy Bailey

MEMOS FOR MYSTICS

BY ELSA JOY BAILEY

First Mystics of the World Edition 2014
Published by Mystics of the World
ISBN-13: 978-0692209554
ISBN-10: 0692209557
Title ID: 4775779

For information contact:
Mystics of the World
Eliot, Maine
www.mysticsoftheworld.com

Cover graphics by Margra Muirhead
Artwork in manuscript by Elsa Joy Bailey
Printed by CreateSpace
Available from Mystics of the World and Amazon.com

For Tom and Jeannie, Dave and Nina,
whose presence in my life is an endless blessing.

For the countless dear friends and teachers who have
helped to open my mind and heart.

For Denice and Ginny, whose loving support and
caring brought this book into being.

And for you, the seekers who walk beside me, though we
have never met.

If you want to dance with God today,
say hello to an earthworm;
kiss a flower;
eat a bowl of happiness.

—Elsa Joy Bailey

CONTENTS

PREFACE

It is one of life's great paradoxes that becoming aware of our spiritual nature is as important as breath itself; yet there is nothing easy about a spiritual practice. Indeed, it is possibly the most difficult discipline known to man. And why is that? Partly because, unlike piano lessons and weight lifting, the results are often subtle and private rather than open and obvious. And, most importantly, because while worldly disciplines enhance our ego, a spiritual practice in fact leads to the ego's disappearance. None of us, at the start of our work, greet that fact with much joy.

Recall how you feel about waking up at dawn for a meeting at the office, and you will know how most sleeping angels feel about being prodded awake.

And yet, sooner or later, many of us come to realize that a spiritual practice is not only vital, but urgent. After all, the Truth is true—we are Spirit, we are angels—and to point our minds in line with the Truth is our only door to freedom. A grasshopper can pretend it's a daffodil for as long as it wants—but it cannot grow petals or live a peaceful life standing still in the grass. Equally, we can go about pretending we are small, weak, perishable physical creatures—but it will never amount to a hill of beans. Because in fact we are something else: we are Spirit.

These letters are personal notes of support and love written from one sleeping angel to all the others who walk beside her on the path home to God.

—Elsa Joy Bailey

These memos are a hug and a high five to everyone who is putting authentic effort and true grit into awakening. Because, despite the inevitable pitfalls and potholes and slippery-when-wet moments, this work we are doing day by day by day is quite simply the most important work on earth.

—*Elsa Joy Bailey*

ANT STORY

"You know," said an ant to his best friend, "It has come to my attention that life isn't really much fun. Have you noticed it? All we do is work, work, work; build, build, build; lift, lift, lift; labor, labor, labor; crawl, crawl, crawl."

"We're doing what we were born to do," replied his friend. "And look here—you're not supposed to ask questions like that. Questions disturb the order of things."

"Well, even so, I am asking questions," said the first ant.

"You'll have to leave the group," whispered his friend. "It won't do to have you complaining like this. You'll upset the other ants."

So the first ant went away and found a quiet place all to himself, where he meditated on the mysteries of life. After a long, long, long while he suddenly got a stunning realization—that his ant life was a dream.

"So!" he said. "I'm dreaming I am an ant. Well, there it is! I better go back and live out my ant dream in peace."

So he returned to his old family and took up the very same ant chores he had done before he left.

In short order, his old friend spotted him and said, "You're back! How nice that you came to your senses! See, you're a normal ant now like the rest of us, busy working."

The ant replied, "Yes, I came to my senses, all right. But I'm not the same ant, not at all."

"What do you mean?" asked his friend. "How have you changed?"

"Well," said the ant, "when I thought I was an ant, life was just plain hard work. But then I discovered I was dreaming, and now my life feels like something far, far different—an adventure."

WHAT IS LOVE?

It's the substance of you, the substance of me.
But *what* is it?

Words are helpless; words can only hint. We
don't know what It is; we only know *that* It is.
Which is enough.

Love is what springs when you're looking in
the other direction; what rushes in when your
definitions drop away. When you absolutely don't
know anything whatsoever anymore, *there It is*—
painting Itself madly across your life with sudden
strokes and unexpectedly rash ink.

Love follows no rules; has no uniform
behavior; cannot be contained in a jar.

Love is what happens when you disappear
into thin air. Then It's the ground holding up your
feet; the rain scrubbing the trees; a flower sneezing
perfume; opulent sun; the brilliance of a child's
eyes; warm fingers, warm toes; a lover wrapping
you up in a twenty-pound smile; hot cocoa on an
ice cold night. It's music, It's silence; It's an old
rubber band that accidentally falls out in the shape
of a heart.

But don't think Love is all yeses and no noes
—Love walks backward near anger; It refuses to
chat with bleakness or density; and It vanishes
entirely when you try to box It in. Love is smarter
than all of us put together.

Make a deal with yourself now to forget everything you ever knew about Love; It never cares what you think anyway.

Just give It breathing room. If you sense It's hanging around, shut up and listen. Because Love is the God within hurling Itself into your world to sweeten the pictures. It heals, It creates, It comforts, It unites. Often It removes the unnecessary. Yes, and It can heat up parts of you that are dead from neglect, if you don't question Its methods. We see a kiss and say *that's Love*, but the truth is, Love is Love and the kiss is a poor shadow on the wall trying to live up to the Real Thing.

One more time: Love is what happens when you disappear into thin air. Disappear as fast as you can—you won't miss the weight. Afterwards, you'll watch Love float you into sanity, into realness, into vision. Then, with Love as your lens, you can collect smiles like flowers and hold them alive in your heart.

Oh yes you can.

WHO ARE YOU?

Life being so wondrously circular, you've probably already heard the delicious teacup question which Zen masters over the years have put to their prize students. Here is a valuable teacup, rimmed in gold and hand-painted by a consummate artist. What, asks the teacher, is the most valuable part of this cup?

And I am sure you know the answer. *Voila!* The most valuable part is the empty space within, that which permits the cup to hold tea — to function.

Now that seems simple enough to us, doesn't it? Easy to grasp. And yet, look how often we forget our most valuable inward part and mistake ourself for the teacup! Then, imagining ourself to be a small, helpless piece of clay, we find ourselves cut off from the silent Living Substance from which issues all blessings, all nourishment, all functioning, all life.

And what does it take for us to be hypnotized into a perception of littleness? Not much — a simple headache can do it. An ache, a pain, a sad headline — and within seconds I can imagine myself to be a flawed teacup. As such, I not only appear to be separate from all other teacups, but my view has now dwindled down to seeing life, and myself, as dark and endangered.

Yet the moment I become conscious of my oneness with the invisible Life that undergirds and informs all that is—what a serenely different view now opens up before me!

Because if "All That Is" is who I Am, it follows that I am one with the cup, one with the tea, one with the table, and one with the infinite sea of Spirit which links all of these into one indissoluble whole. Only from that perspective can I see I am not small, fragile, finite—which is why it is such a terribly vital realization.

In fact, I cannot truly be alive until I see past this tiny, insubstantial teacup in front of me. When, in some luminous moment, I see I am one with that Spirit which creates and supports and surrounds all vessels, what is left for me to fear? What is left for me to want? There is no me to fear. There is no me to want.

Now, here, forever, there is only one thing— Omnipresence.

Yielding

Somewhere along the line, most of you have probably seen one of those ingenious stone tumbling machines at work. I hope you have—they're incredible. Pebbles of all sizes and shapes are placed inside a simple container; next you turn on a switch and the container begins rocking back and forth in a slow circular motion, forcing the stones to be shuffled one against another, over and over and over again. There is a soft monotonous chatter going on as this happens; the stones appear to abrade and jostle each other with easy abandon.

This intimate dance of stones continues all day, all night, all week, all month, all year. Yes, yes, that's how long it takes for the abrading, the rubbing, the tumbling to do its magic. If you were to stand urgently by the machine for a weekend and wait for a quick result, you would be deeply disappointed. One weekend is a mere blink in the polishing process. This is a long, long trip the stones are taking; it requires your most profound patience and respect. And if you are able to endure the passage of time without wincing, if you are able to listen to the low, ceaseless murmur of dancing pebbles, if you are able to relax and let the gleaming unfold in its own slow inexorable way, in the end you find yourself the recipient of an amazing gift.

And I mean amazing. After endless months of non-stop, shoulder-to-shoulder roughhousing and cavorting, you approach the machine, turn off the motor, place a few stones in your hand.

And what have you got? Open the fingers. There they are: gems with rough edges, barbs, and dullness gone forever. Here is what remains: essence of stone.

Deeply burnished, glistening like fire, impossibly flawless stones are now warming the skin of your palm. You can't bear to put them down; they are too sleek and beautiful.

And you stand there stunned, because no matter how much beauty you've seen before, you simply can't get over this one single miracle. Before they were simply ordinary stones; now they are priceless.

So the next time you tumble against a cloudy day, an edgy friend, a staggering debt, a hot dry patch of insult, or a wild burst of illness, remember the stones. Tell yourself: I will surrender to this tumbling and polishing and rest myself in the One who controls the switch.

Because I am being polished. I am being shaved of self. I am being reduced to essence.

I am being made a pure stone in the hand of God.

PEACE

There is no surprise like the surprise of Peace. It's as startling as a moonbeam visible at high noon. How It operates is beyond me. I only know It is reliable if I am reliable—if I remember to stop and call to It when the trees are upside down and the birds have quit singing.

It's reliable and It's food, yet there's nothing routine about It, ever.

Time after time I have paused to call on Peace when I had no idea what shape Peace would take and what It might say when It got there. Peace has, in fact, no standard answers—have you noticed that? It is as unpredictable as jumping beans. All we can observe is that when we do open the door to invite It in, It is always right on the money, always perfect in Its response.

I remember a particular day when everything in life seemed to be going awry. Somehow I had tumbled deep into a pool of disorder. To say it another way, I found myself looking at things as they seemed and no further. How they seemed was chaotic.

So it went along in this manner for a while, me walking on slippery ground, until out of nowhere I suddenly felt an impulse towards sanity.

The impulse settled on me like a friendly hand, straightening my windblown cap with a quick tap. Following that tap, I spent an entire day meditating on order, on peace. I made it my day's work. Putting everything human, everything me aside, I simply called to Peace. And called to It. And called to It. And what happened during that day? Nothing.

But ...

By the next morning, all the world seemed slower and softer and less dangerous. Mysteriously, I began cleaning out closets and neatening the house. Something heavy had lifted out of my awareness. And in its place, there It was, a subtle but tangible No-Thing with Its own faint fragrance and a distinct hum—Peace.

No, I don't know how It does that, but It does. It floats into our presence like a surprise summer mist. Moistening the dry spots, calming the tides, combing the tangles, feeding the hungers.

I've seen It come a thousand and one times, and still it is a mystery. It probably always will be. All I know is, without It, I'm nothing.

HEAVEN HAS NO WALLS

Waterfalls flashing, leaping down a descent of canyon rocks, can hold no sticks, no leaves, no thoughts, no history, no sameness—no nothing. The water races along in stark immediacy. It has one choice—to be new in each instant.

God is like that, utterly still, yet flawlessly new and moving. Don't ask how that is possible; none of us knows. It just is the way It is. And if we can summon the courage to ride with It, all of joy rises to greet us.

Before we met Silence, most of us operated in the same way: we enclosed our histories and limits in our arms and tried to stumble forward, or at least sideways, under their weight. Often we were proud of these loads; they gave us character and substance, so we thought. And that's not all; so infatuated is this world with tragedy that whole dances have been created to celebrate graceful moves under private burdens. High honors are given to the imprisoned beings who are fleet of step, who are strong under fire.

So for many of us it was a blow, at first, to discover there are no awards offered by God for tragedy; even more insulting to find there is no such category in that Presence.

It's true—heaven is tragedy-blind. However! Here's the good news: those few who do break free from prison receive Ecstasy Itself.

And knowing that Ecstasy is a prize worth wearing, we keep on with the work. The very tough work. For we discover that to ride the divine waters, we must let go of our most prized possessions: sad little histories, communal madness, narrow prisons, and socially approved sufferings.

And with all of that gone, Who is left?

It makes us tremble. Invariably, in the process of opening our hands and soul to let yesterday's suffering drift away, we encounter temporary fear about our sudden weightlessness. How will I move? How will I swim? How will I know where to go, when to turn? What on earth do I do next?

Questions without an answer.

Questions without an answer, because no answer is necessary. Riding the divine waters requires no map, no guide, no reference, no tools. And, most of all, no past. A past weighs us down, makes us too heavy to rest featherlike on the stunningly light current.

Riding the divine waters requires but one quality—surrender.

Notice I didn't say surrender was an easy thing to do. It's not. But it is possible. Remember that! It's been done and done, and you will do it, and I will do it. Why will we do it? *Because we must.*

There is no past in God, and if we wish to know the inexpressible joy of floating in His arms (and who among us does not?) then first we must surrender our poor, gray, ghostly past.

Get to work.

THE OPENING

The very first time I sat down to meditate, it felt like being in the dentist's chair. Actually for the first many, many attempts it felt that way. My nose itched, my legs seemed leaden; I was asquirm, hoping to be done with it. When the time was over, my body literally raced upright, like a prisoner released on bail. Had I been graded on these early efforts, the mark would have been F minus.

Yet I persisted, because something deep within me knew it was imperative that I continue. Waking up cannot occur while our attention is fixed, slavelike, on the screen of the external world. In our normal ego state that is precisely where we are staring; we are in a trance.

So I would come to the dreaded exercise in silence, prodded from within and hating it. I did not tell anyone about this agony of resistance, because I didn't want to be marked a failure. But privately I was certain I was hopelessly backward as a spiritual apprentice. I brought my flawed and resisting body along and willed it through its paces. Eyes closed, my mind would jump from thought to thought to thought like a mad leapfrog. Everything in me wanted the meditation to be over, and somewhere an imaginary eye kept consulting an imaginary watch. Week after week, month after month, I kept trying. It was a comedy, really—me fighting off God. The battle went on like that for about eight months. Far from bringing peace, each and every meditation was a lesson in misery.

Then! One day, like a feather cutting through cement, Something suddenly took over my meditation. One second I was noticing an itch on my neck, and in the next—for no reason whatso-ever—a Presence rose up and engulfed me in a huge unearthly smile. All resistance melted away like vapor and all there was left was the Smile. I was swimming in it. I floated on its waves, a cork bobbing up and down on Love.

When I finally opened up my eyes, a ghost of the smile still remained. My mind was incredulous—I knew full well I had done nothing to earn such a gift! Yet there it was—it had happened. Following this experience, I looked on meditation in an entirely new light. I now saw becoming still as an immense luxury, even though at first I had no idea if I would ever be revisited by the Smile. To my complete amazement and joy, I discovered the Smile would return whenever I entered the Silence. To this day, It is still with me—It shows up each time I get still, and sometimes even during the day, when my eyes are open and I think of God.

Meditate. Meditate even if you dislike it, and do it daily. It tells the Presence you are ready.

REMOVING THE BLOCKS

Well, let's get truthful here—*how much Love can you take?*

Understand, I'm not talking about *You*. You *are* Love. So You can take lots of Love; actually, quarts of it, liters of it, infinite tankfuls. Love is Your very breath.

So, no, I don't mean You. But if we're talking about our old friend the human ego (and we are), the answer is, not much. Haven't you noticed? The ego abhors Love—and with good reason, for Love's presence leaves it with absolutely nothing to do, nowhere to go, no one to be. In fact, nothing describes the dynamics of our human world better (or more deliciously) than Murphy's Law, which is why we all laugh so hard when we hear it. You remember Murphy's Law: Whatever can possibly go wrong, will!

You bet. In the three-dimensional world of form and effect, things going wrong is status quo. The material world, after all, is a tangle of nonsense built entirely from vapor—that is, from the notion of separation from God. With "separation" as its base, what else but things going wrong could possibly follow? And follow and follow and follow.

Which is why day after day, year after year, decade after decade, century after century, we find humans looking frantically around for a way to fix it all up. Fixing things up is ice cream to the human mind; it gives it a sense of purpose. Even better, it gives it another way to distract you.

Distract you from what? From asking the right questions: *what dream is fixable*? How, since a dream is built out of sheer vapor, can you possibly correct it? Can you mend vapor? Get it to stay put? Make it do what you want? Curl its hair? Send it to the store? Teach it to behave?

You've tried it; you know the answer.

Trying it, and trying it, and trying it again is how, finally, you came to realize the truth. That the only way to deal with Murphy's Law is to put it back down on the table, empty your hands, close your eyes, and sink deep, deeper, deepest into the place where Murphy's Law does not apply, now or ever—in Silence.

And what do You find there? You guessed it: Infinite Love—which means everything but Murphy.

Bon voyage.

ABANDONING LITTLENESS

Sooner or later it becomes clear that to believe you are nothing more than a limited human is to live a crippled life.

It's nothing personal; all of us start out thus informed. The belief of separateness and limitation is universal, handed freely (alas, even eagerly!) to everyone who enters this world. It is a given.

And oh, what a terrible gift it is! With one quick thrust to the mind, this belief cuts each of us into dwarfhood. And there we stay.

Of course, the shape and cut of your set of limitations will vary from mine. But the end result is the same: separateness is separateness no matter what color it is painted. And limitations are limitations are limitations. So, yes, we all start out even-steven, being fed on milk, gruel, and mis-information. Our problem is this: that what we have learned seems so sane! *So readily do we accept the notion of separation that we fail to notice the entire concept is awry.*

That's the way of the world. We all share in it. And so it goes, until one day, somewhere along the road, someone or something hints to us we are mistaken, that our basic premise is grievously false.

Some of us pursue the hint. We pick up the slight thread and trace it slowly, slowly, back to the Truth—that we are not who we seem. Our facts have been misreported. Far from being meaningless wisps in a wayward and cruel planet, we are something far, far more. We are Spirit. We are Love. We are limitless.

"What?" we say. *"Can this be true?"* For clearly this new vision does not sit well with our initial view of us-ness.

Some will fall away at this point; the discrepancy between the world of the human and the world of the Spirit seems too fearful to contemplate. Others of us tumble forward; for some inexplicable reason an interior voice has whispered that the Truth is true.

And if it has, we begin the struggle of reordering our life, our thoughts, our practice to conform to this new, odd Vision of Things.

So far, so good. But why, why does it seem so hard to make the shift? Here's why: it seems hard because the old system, however cruel and constricting, is comfortable, and our addiction to comfort is legendary.

This is why teachers so often remind us that problems are our friends; discomfort is the prod which can (if we let it) push us away from our odd attraction to separation and death and into a new, living alliance with What Is.

Do not despair if you see you are still loyal to the old order. Do as the elders tell us: Pay attention. Pay attention. Pay attention—*Noticing heals.*

THREE LEAVES

I have in my hand three separate leaves that I picked up from their previous home on the street and brought inside. One is decorated with little feathers spun out of rust, bursting out of its center spine. Another is a splash of pure gold. And the last one is brown, with two of its edges turned upwards in a makeshift grin.

They don't look remotely alike, yet they are all leaves, family members. Which one is best? An absurd question, clearly. All of them are best. Or to be more accurate, there is no best; each leaf danced on a perfect tree, offered dollops of live, luscious color to the world for a mystical while, and then floated down slowly to go to sleep on a bed of green velvet.

So we're like that, too—leaves of varying shapes and colors and textures feeding off tree sap and bowing into breezes until we're ready to break off and fall away. The difference is, we've got minds, which enables us to label ourselves different. Once we are classified as different, we have tree wars. Our tree is better than the next tree, and our shapes are classier and more savvy than the shapes over there in the next yard, which entitles us to feel proud. Or else the shapes over there in the next yard are classier and more savvy than we are, in which case we hang our heads.

We find all of this constant comparison fascinating, of course, but it makes it easy to forget that we're all leaves, no more, no less. And if we focus on the difference in shape and color, we may not find out anything about the nature of leaves themselves and the nature of life. We may miss the point.

So that's the message behind "never judge a book by its cover," which we have been hearing for years and years and still don't pay much attention to. We like judging books by their covers; it's quicker than reading the whole thing. And we like calling person "A" worthwhile and person "B" absurd. Again, it's easier than looking deeper and wider.

I have in my hand three leaves, all different. One is gold, one is rust, one is brown. You may have one you prefer, so may I. Nevertheless, they're all best in their own way, and each one of them point ceaselessly to the miracle of life itself.

A Perfect Day

Have you ever had a day that is all grunge and growl and no ice cream cones? Sure you have; so have I. Let me tell you about one of mine.

What I remember most about this particular day is that nothing seemed to fit. The morning arrived too early. I overcame that, but when I arrived at work I was given a new assignment which was impossibly unappealing and awkward, something I plain didn't want to do. And everyone in the office seemed sour, as though they'd over-dosed on lemonade. I did close my eyes briefly to remember they were holy creatures, but it was a cursory overture. When I opened my eyes, people were still futzing around in an unhappy way and the harmony was, well, absent.

I began doing the unfortunate assignment, sighing heavily the way people do when they think happiness is an entirely alien concept.

By lunch I was ready for help. I took my cafeteria tray outside, found a bench under a tree and sat there alone, watching a troop of high-energy ants march meaningfully along the edge of a cement curb. I noticed that to an ant, nearly everything is an obstacle. After all, they're miniscule.

My spot under the tree was very peaceful, and eventually I began to wonder why I had spent all morning looking at life with such small eyes. I thought, look at this! When the ego is in play, our vision is as small as ant eyes staring at pebbles and seeing boulders. That's exactly what I had been doing: staring at pebbles and seeing boulders.

So I closed my eyes and remembered that the bench, the tree, the ants, the day, the office, the work were not outside of me, controlling me; they were contained within my infinite Self.

I decided to accept them as innocent.

When I went back upstairs to my desk, I was wearing different eyes—no judging, no blaming, no searching for molehills to make into mountains. No peering at events through a frown. No squinting.

It is a far, far easier way to look at things. As I removed the strictures from my seeing, everything around me seemed to sigh and relax and settle into a cool, easy pace.

Later that afternoon, someone in our group decided, on a whim, to go get ice cream for everyone. So towards the end of the day, there we all were, scooping out heaping platefuls of ice-cold joy, joshing and kidding around with each other as though we were all twelve and it was recess.

I thanked the ants for the lesson.

WHAT TO DO TODAY

We hear so many questions about life purpose, life calling, life work. What should I be
doing? What is holy? What isn't? What does God
want me to do?

It's not nearly as complicated as we'd like to
make it. Your purpose is to do exactly what you're
doing right now; the assignment is to change the
way you view it.

Instead of grumping through the day (as we
all have done, trust me) we have the opportunity
to change our entire scenario by moving through
it with a blessing, touching everyone and everything we meet with a quick, silent feather brush of
love. In other words, it's not really important what
you're doing; it's the way you're doing it that
counts.

It's kind of hard for us to believe that. We
think holy work isn't holy work unless it falls into
the category of overt healing and helping. For
example, if we're not working for Mother Teresa,
we assume our functioning cannot possibly be
divine. But we're dead wrong about that—it is
never the nature of our work, but rather the nature
of our heart that determines our spiritual muscle.

And I don't mean to say we are not sometimes
led from one employment to another, or guided to
shift from this task to that one, because indeed this

kind of alteration and changeover does occur. When a change of this sort leads to an endeavor that is gentler or kinder or happier than the one you have now, wonderful.

In the meantime, however, here you are, and here is your world, and here are the chores and people you've been given for this moment. Whatever they are, they're your present assignment. The adventure is to look for the Light within everything, right now.

I remember a morning some time ago when I had a lengthy errand to run and I didn't want to do it. On top of that, the day was unbearably hot and I felt cross about that. Actually, I was displeased with the entire day, period. It wasn't going the way I wanted it to. Some days are like that.

So I realized I was on treacherous ground, primed and ready to have a ruinous day. On my way out the door, I plucked up a lovely tape of spiritual music, put it in a Walkman and began playing songs of love into my head. One of the lyrics said, "*I bless you brother, for you are one with me.*" I played the tape all the way to my destination and all the way back home. The errand turned out to be ridiculously simple; it became 20 degrees cooler thanks to a healing coastal breeze. Everyone I met on my journey was amazingly nice; I might even say delightful.

Being one with my brother put me in so gentle a state that even my hair was smiling. People looked like little angels bobbing along the sidewalks. Traffic noise was curiously like music. Nothing was out of place. Nothing. The day had become a kind of secret ice cream cone.

So that's the assignment. Change your view. And there, right inside the same old-same old, we discover that nameless place where, Surprise!— heaven is hiding.

ENTRANCE REQUIREMENT

She was wearing her favorite ivory silk chiffon and she felt just fine. Leaving the body had been easier than she expected; why had there been no pain? she wondered.

Well, never mind—she was here now, right where she belonged. She was perched neatly in a straight-backed chair in a small, warmly lit foyer. Hands folded, she waited for her appointment with the usher.

Never before had she felt so grateful for all her hard work as a Christian—the years of Bible study, fasting, prayer, self-denial, avoiding TV and movies, her pure vegetarian diet. How lucky she was to have that record behind her! She shifted slightly in her chair, settling comfortably against its hard straight back.

When the usher appeared, a medium-sized man wearing a simple white robe, she sat up instantly with an expectant smile. At last—her moment of reward!

"Great news!" said the usher warmly. "You're going straight into the pre-heaven seminar."

"Wonderful," she said, standing up. "I can't wait!" As she followed the usher down a long broad hallway, she quietly confided her happy anticipations.

"I've been going over and over scriptures in my mind while I sat waiting," she whispered to the usher, "and I'm quite certain I can answer any questions they present."

"Well, this isn't exactly a seminar on the Bible, ma'am," said the usher. He smiled, and his deep brown eyes crinkled slightly at the corners.

"Oh?" She was taken aback. "No questions on the Bible?"

"Not exactly," replied the usher. He paused in front of a large handsome oak door, opened it up and motioned her inside. "Here we are," he said encouragingly.

She entered the room, stared, and then stopped cold.

It was a palatial setting. Taking command of the room was a long mahogany dining table, laid out with painstaking care. A lake of lavish flowers bordered by tall lean candles formed the centerpiece. And seated at the table, in resplendent high-backed chairs, were numerous guests dressed in evening clothes. At the serving end of the table perched a huge, succulent roast, surrounded by what looked like candied yams. Small bowls of premium chocolate were placed at each setting, nested beside fine crystal goblets holding fine wine. Hand-painted porcelain containers filled with cigars and cigarettes were placed at even intervals along the exquisite lace tablecloth. At the table's end stood a pitcher of high-cholesterol eggnog. And a few feet away from the table, beaming down on the guests like a giant watchful eye, was a large wall-mounted television screen. It was broadcasting vivid pictures of a political massacre in South America.

She was stunned. Her entire body froze. She found to her horror she could not even move her feet. Gently, the usher helped her over to her appointed seat. Her fellow guests barely looked up. They sipped wine and chatted amiably, waving away brief gusts of smoke with their hands. Occasionally a burst of laughter rose up like a kite and hovered over the table. Gunshots echoed from the TV.

Eyes wide, face white, hands clenched in a knot, she turned to the usher. "How can you possibly put me in a place like this? I have refused alcohol and meat and tobacco and sweets and TV for the last twenty years! What kind of cruel joke is this? I deplore this room! It disgusts me!"

"Oh, yes," said the usher kindly, "that's why you're here. You see, in heaven there is no fear allowed. This little exercise in meat and mayhem is being held to free you of your disgust."

"But that's monstrously unfair!" she cried, trying to control the tears sneaking into her throat. "And I suppose my husband, who guzzled hot dogs and beer and watched war films every day of his life—I suppose you've raced him into heaven straightaway?"

"Oh, no, of course not," said the usher. "He's in the pre-heaven class, just like you."

"Well, he's certainly not here," she snapped, waving her hand over at the assembled dinner guests.

"That's right, he's not," said the usher, enfolding the distraught woman in a soothing smile. "He's next door at the all-vegetable table, listening to a Bach cantata."

IF YOU HATE IT, IT'S GOTCHA

Remember when you were a kid and one of your siblings suddenly saw you as a perfect object of torture?

Well, maybe you never had that experience. I did. And I know someone else who did; but in this case it was someone who found a miracle cure for it. We'll call her Alice.

Her brother liked to tickle Alice silly, having discovered that she hated it. For the first several tickling episodes she did what any sane child will do: she fought and kicked and bit and hollered for Mother. This delighted her brother to no end; having found a new and rewarding hobby, he persisted in his surprise attacks.

But one day the victim made up her mind she would put an end to the torture; and she would do it by refusing to respond. Through sheer force of will she remained still as a statue the next time her brother initiated a tickling ordeal; he went away profoundly disgruntled.

Of course, he didn't give up. He returned later that day and tried again. Taking a deep, strong breath, this indomitable child steeled herself to remain perfectly still and inert throughout the teasing. Her brother stomped off in a huff, feeling baffled. Four more times he made an attempt to undo his sister's stone-faced demeanor. Four times he failed. After that, he lost all interest in tickling and never bothered his sister again.

That's discipline. That's true grit. And it's a great, great lesson for all of us on how to meet the dings and pings in life that annoy us, rattle us, drive us nuts. The lesson is: stop responding.

I don't mean be a fake. I don't mean swallow your suffering and paste a slick smile on your face. I mean reach in and call on your courage. Alice, when she decided to ward off her brother's tickling, summoned all her gut strength and rose above her instinct to squeal.

So that's what I mean. Employ some of the same staunch discipline Alice used to remain unmoved by whatever is tickling your anger button. When you see you are slipping off center and into a pool of dislike, expend effort to stay centered and calm. You have, we all have, a place of peace within us, whose waters are never shut down. Go there. Borrow from it. Refuse to cave; refuse to slide into reaction. Whatever it is that is stirring you up will eventually get tired of no payoff and leave you alone. No kidding.

And along with your effort to sidestep reactivity, there is another smart move. Take a good look at the situation that is arousing you, and then send it packing by withdrawing all judgment about it. Kill it with compassion. Hatred is a powerful energy; it attracts the objects of its fancy. So if you don't want to attract a dismal situation over and over and over again, give up the luxury of hating it. Blanket it with good will; it will lose interest in you in short order.

DON'T BLAME YOU

Not now.

Not ever.

No matter what.

Let's get very clear about this. The airplane crash, the crime wave, the tornado, the recession, the dread disease: *they are not your fault*.

In truth, they're not even there. Period.

Here's what they are—images. Pictures of separation which rise and fall across the screen of the human mind like bits of fluff scattered by the wind. We all have that human mind; pictures will flit across it every day. Don't blame you.

Don't blame you, because pictures are sourced by the joint human mind, operating from its shared belief in separation. All pictures, all appearances, are symptoms of that belief. And as any doctor can tell you, your best chance of recovery is to go after the belief itself, rather than wrestle with its symptoms.

Yet we do wrestle, don't we? How often we get caught up by guilt when some dark picture presents itself in our life. "Why am I failing? Why am I lonely? Why am I sick?"

You're not.

You are His Holy Son—perfect, pure, complete, and deathless—No kidding.

So stop blaming. You are not responsible for random *images*. You do have a task, though, and here's what it is: to remember the images are images—not reality—and then *to avoid falling for them.*

Resist the temptation to give these pictures power, and you have discovered the secret of Freedom.

But *wait*! How do you withdraw power from a picture of darkness?

Here's how: by remembering who you are— Who you are really. When the world has been tucked into bed (with all of its dazzle and dance and dire doings) and all is quiet—*Who are you now*? Remember that, and you will remember that I Am is the one constant behind all world appearances. I Am is the one and only power. I Am is the only Life alive. And It does not fray, because It has no seams.

Call to That.

Let the appearances alone. They can't last. How can lifeless pictures last? They can't. Unless, of course, you invite them to dinner.

Don't do that!

SEEING STRAIGHT

There was a toy I cherished when I was a kid. Maybe you had one, too—a kaleidoscope.

Peering intently through one end, I would focus its fragmented lens on some object and watch it unfold into a spectacle of glorious shapes and colors. O, rapture! The images, dazzling beyond belief, moved and shifted in perfect concert with my rotating lens. Endless delights! Endless hues formed themselves out of this deliberately broken lens. Yet, remove the lens, and instantly! the object was whole once again. And of course, it always had been. The lens had misreported.

I thought I had lost that small, bewitching toy a long time ago.

But no, I hadn't. In due time it came to me I still possessed a kaleidoscope that was built-in— my own human eyes. Could it be true? How I believed in those eyes! Trusted their news reports. Relied on their data. Rallied to their cause!

Until one day, aided by beloved teachers, assisted by Grace, the truth became inescapable: my human eye was a hopelessly distorted lens through which the perfect One appears shredded into fragments. Day in, day out, it issues a landscape of separate bits of form and color— endless images of pain, endless images of pleasure. Images so compelling, so fascinating, that for years they held my gaze captive. For oh so long I had used this lens in perfect confidence. Making decisions based on its findings. Acting on its reports.

And all the time it was a wrong prescription.

Yet the realization that worldly images (and the "me" that sees them) are distortions was only my first step in learning how to see. After that began the task of retraining my focus; undoing my faith in human sense. Talk about a rigorous class!

I have learned to walk slower in this world; to pause a hundred times a day. The pausing gives me space to refocus when, day by day, minute by minute, I am issued bulletins from my faulty human lens. In that pausing, I can turn my gaze inward and lean hard on the source of perfect vision—the immaculate Eye of God.

And that inner vision, as we all know, is the only vision that is not blind.

EASY DOES IT

One of the kindest things about God is the fact that He never rushes us.

He Who Knows All clearly senses that as we begin our waking up, we are far too frightened to give up being us all at once. No, we clutch our ego self to our bosom like a treasured rag doll we have sworn never, ever to throw away.

I heard a true story once about a family of war orphans who were brought to this country by a loving couple who wanted to raise and nurture them as their own. When the children debarked from the boat, the couple rushed forward with hearts open wide and offered each child a luscious ice cream cone. The children, who had endured years of torture and deprivation, looked at the cones uncertainly. Finally, the eldest boy took a tentative bite ... and then threw it down on the ground, whispering to his brothers and sisters: "Don't eat it! Don't eat it!—*They're trying to freeze our tongues!*"

Fear is blind. When I heard that story, I thought—how many times have I done the same thing! How many times have I darkened my sight by seasoning it with suspicion? Have put my faith in how things seem rather than how things are?

God is Good, God is Love, all the awakened ones have told us. And yet as soon as we realize we must discard ourselves in order to experience that Love, how often resistance rises up in us! How often moments come when we drop God flat on the floor, crying, "He's trying to freeze out me!"

Oh, countless times! And here's the funny part: He *is* trying to freeze out me, because me is my only problem!

In my own walk toward God, I have often had the sense of moving slowly, slowly out of a cold, dark place into the "Sun." And step by step, as the heat from the Within grows more intense, I find I am shedding the heavy garments of my old self, my old life, my old identity. It's not a planned thing, really. They seem to drop off without fanfare as I move ever deeper into His warmth.

Yet even though I rejoice at the delicious lightness that follows useless things dropping away, here's the fact: I know full well I could not, at the start, have discarded my apparel all at once. To be naked before God without preparation would have terrified me. I walk toward Him as is, and Grace peels away all that is false.

Slowly, slowly is my pace. And I have no doubt that one day all of my garments, habits, concepts—all the "me" paraphernalia—will fade gently away, as all dreams must. Then, only then, wearing God alone as my sole garment, will I express perpetual Peace.

WAKING UP IS SO HARD TO DO

Suppose we all woke up tomorrow and discovered the spiritual life was easy? I mean socks-off, swing-on-a-porch easy.

Wouldn't that be a landscape of May mornings, all moist and bright and bursting with flowers? There would be this one shocking moment of sudden awareness, and forever after you would walk on gilded ground, with pocketfuls of angel glow to soften your steps and dismantle all obstacles. Tough times would fly by like dust mites on a spring breeze.

No more knots to untie. No more lessons. No more setbacks. No more falling into potholes and climbing back out. No more days ripped open at the seams. Heaven.

But it doesn't happen that way. To any of us. Why? Because there's something around here that doesn't want us to be walking the path. Our ego.

So that means those of us waking up to Spirit have a daily chore to do. We're here to heal our minds of the ego. And the ego is much like one of those hot viruses they're talking about—alien, invasive, aggressive, out to kill. Can it kill the Self? Never. Can it cause trouble? Sure it can, if we let it.

And we do. Discarding the ego is not a quickie adventure. It takes time, patience, care, guts, and relentless compassion. (And if you've got all of those on hand, please send me a quart—stat!)

A virus extends its life by finding a host cell in which it can sit, feed, live, and duplicate itself endlessly. The ones that have been bursting out of the rain forests recently have done especially violent work when they latched onto human cells. Killer work.

Our ego virus works the same way. The ego is a thought of separation—aggressive, invasive, fraudulent. The ego insists it is a separate and finite entity, and if you accept its premise, that's what you think you are, too.

Don't feel you are at fault. Here in the material dimension, we're born with this virus. We're trained from childhood to learn and relearn that we are separate little packages—applauded for it, in fact. That's the ego holding its ground. The virus clutching onto its host cells.

So surrounded are we by this errant thought of division that for most of us it takes years to even question its validity. We spend a long, long time thinking we are nothing more than these lovable specks, born to die. And since our virus has invaded every aspect of the world around us, its principles are reinforced at every turn.

Until we jump ship. And then, when we finally begin our walk Home, a battle starts in earnest. It's no different, really, than the war between an immune system and a burgeoning flu.

The ego within us rails at the sacred within us and begins screaming for more attention and space. As part of its battle plan, it presents obstacles— reams of them, gobs of them, all with an eye to distracting us from proceeding Homeward.

But you can't fix your gaze egoward and Homeward at the same time, so each moment that the ego succeeds in dragging our eye toward its system of chaos and separation, it wins the battle of that moment. Make no mistake—the ego is exquisitely clever.

Conversely, each instant that we spend looking within towards God is a knife in the belly of the ego, because any moment that we are one with our Real Self, the ego—which is simply an errant thought—ceases to exist; and when we reach a point of living from the Self, the ego ceases forever.

It's the distance between these first brief en- counters with Oneness and the state of living there that comprises the path. A long path, because our belief in division has deep, strong roots.

And fighting off the "me" virus is part of the territory. *Of course* it's hard work. The virus may be a mirage, but while we're staring into it and under its spell, *it's got teeth.*

LOSING OUR BAGGAGE

By now we've all noticed it. Each time an upset occurs in our life, there's one person always present to witness it. And every darn time, it's the same person. Me.

Myself is always present to witness an upset. Wait! I don't mean the large, luminous Spirit Self whose very essence is peace. Not that Self.

I mean our small, dense, finite, historical self, the one who believes it was born with thin hair and weak teeth and endured bad toilet training, and thus grew up to be a mass of nerves and neurotic wirings. I mean the false identity we all receive when we first climb on board Planet Earth, and then (until we catch on that we are something else) proceed to carry around with us everywhere. That self. The one that often feels as heavy and cumbersome as baggage.

No mystery about that; it is baggage. It's five feet so-and-so and weighs a hundred and something pounds; it has a past and a future and inherited tendencies. Its job is to take everything very, very personally. Everything. Which is why it is always present, front and center, during upsets. Because it wants to keep an intensely accurate record of everything that may threaten it; every slight, every injury, every wrongdoing. Keeping records like this takes all day and all night and leaves absolutely no time for self-awareness. That's its plan.

But when we begin to notice, over and over, that that self is the only witness around when unhappiness or chaos sets in, we have begun to catch on to its strategy. Slowly we start to see things right. Without the testimony of that small false self, where is the unhappiness? Where is the difficulty? Where is the injury? Where is the fear?

In other words, if we drop the testimony of this non-credible witness from our mind, what's true will emerge by Itself. And what's true is benign.

Our task is to be alert enough to notice when our ego is attempting to sell us its seeds of fear. We must guard against that, moment by moment by moment. And how do we guard against it? We walk through our day without wearing the heavy, distracting robes of personal sense. We watch whatever happens without looking through the dull lens of judgment. We listen inside without bringing a barrage of opinions to block our hearing.

In short, we lose "me," and gain our Self.

ALL ABOUT NOW

How is this possible? The archery master raises the bow, releases the arrow, and slices it into the bull's-eye dead center. And one thing more: he does it blindfolded.

Sightless, yet successful. What does he have that others don't?

I can see you have the answer already: he has nothing that others don't. What he's doing is using a force that most of us ignore most of the time: now.

For reasons we need not bother to explore at this time, human eyesight is faulty and subject to error. But *now* is a different story. Now is time-free; thus its vision is impeccable. It was impeccable, it is impeccable, it will be impeccable — infinitely.

We have all read tales of how Zen masters conquer archery. Years and years of inner practice brings them to a point of surrender where they can yield totally to the wisdom of the arrow itself. Opening their beings to the heart of This moment, they unite silently with the arrow, and then — they simply allow it to find its way to the target.

We've all done this on occasion; permitted a perfect action to flow through us, untouched by human quirkery. And there is no thrill quite like it. The question is: can we do it again?

Yes! Now stands perpetually at hand, here where you are, ready each moment to unleash its one flawless movement. Our job is to become receded enough to let it emerge.

This sounds so simple, so obvious. And yet we find it hard to do, don't we? We find it hard to do because it is not our habit to live new in each pulse of time.

It is our habit to live mechanically. It is our habit to rest on human memory and reaction. And that's OK. If you see that mechanical movement is what's going on, don't condemn it—notice it. Notice it enough, and eventually it will become apparent that the human mind is mistake-rich and that relying on it alone is a dubious practice. It's a lot like trying to build a fire by rubbing pictures of sticks together when all the time there's a live match sitting in your shirt pocket.

Now is the match in your shirt pocket, ready to blaze, ready to light up your present with its exploding star. Now does precisely what is needed in each given moment—no more, no less. A movement born of Now is exquisite and seamless. All others are counterfeit.

Now works because it is divine. More importantly, now is stunningly accessible.

Use it.

YOU CAN'T HOLD RUNNING WATER IN YOUR FIST

And you can't find God in the letters G, O, D.

Don't get me wrong—I thank God for books. I thank God for teachers. I thank God for tapes. I thank God for all of the countless, priceless symbols that point, point, point to our silent, secret, eternal Self.

Without them, most of us would still be stuck inside five flimsy senses, bemoaning the unfairness of our three-dimensional prison.

But let us never forget that the symbols themselves aren't God—can't be. Books aren't God. Teachers aren't God. Tapes, sand-paintings, statues, candles and stained glass windows aren't God. Even (oh, no!!) crystals aren't God.

What they are, are metaphors; metaphoric images appearing as a sign of our awakening consciousness. But they aren't God Itself. Itself is simply not an object. Not describable. Not capturable. Not anythingable.

And yet, and yet ... we can experience It. Well, let's get blunt. To know God, we *must* experience It, because the healings we witness, the forgiveness that alters us, the harmonies that seem suddenly to emerge on our human landscape, all of these images are formed as a direct result of a God experience.

God is the Living Firelight; the shadows dancing on the walls of our world are hints.

Of course, in this world we select certain objects to hold as sacred. And indeed, perceived through Consciousness, these objects do become imbued with Light. But in the wake of Consciousness, anything can be imbued with Light. All of us remember moments of awareness (out of nowhere) when everything in sight seemed lit with an inner fire. I recall an instance where an ordinary exit sign over a door was totally ablaze with Presence and was able to inform me wordlessly about I Am.

A flash of God will enrapture anything. But without God, even a Bible can be simply an empty form.

Thank God for books.

Thank God for teachers.

Thank God for tapes.

Thank God for music, art, poetry, and every other symbol that whispers of Eternal Spirit. But when you pray, put them all away, these images—all of them—and simply open your heart wide to the Nameless.

May It fill you, stun you, dissolve you through and through with Its unutterable joy.

Making Sense in an Insane World

I wake up one morning and the ants have arrived.

They are in my bedroom: columns of them, menacingly small. Why are they here? Fast and dark and busy, hot in pursuit of their career; bustling their way up the ant ladder. Don't they know they're in the wrong place?

No, they've found a supply of minute crumbs deep in the bowels of the carpet and are now hard at work on highway construction. Thousands of them. So intense, so focused they don't even notice I'm here. To them, I'm like some large distant floating cloud, utterly irrelevant to the task at hand.

I think it's an insane world, and here's proof. I wake up from a dream, planning to meditate — and here's a primal annoyance crawling around under my feet, oozing the confidence that only impossibly large groups can possess.

They're hard at work; I'm planning murder. I buy ant hotels, glue traps, spray — the works. My other plans have dropped into nowhere. This is a goal that requires feverish attention. Using my superior human intellect, I place the poisons wisely and wait for them to take effect. In time, several ants are slain, but this changes nothing.

Thousands more jump in line to take their place. Why are they doing this to me?

Oh! I get it—it's another one of those great, wonderful, lessons the universe is famous for. Am I ready to be illuminated? Yes.

These ants have come to be blessed, and here I am struggling against them, calling them into battle against my giant spray cans and superior wit. But these ants have come to be blessed, and so I walk into another room, where there are no ants to inflame my fears, and settle into the Calm Place that lies hidden behind my uproars. When enough quiet has seeped in, I bless the ants.

Then it comes to me. I remember a friend telling me that nature's finest ant repellent is plain cinnamon. It seems a peaceful enough evacuation device, so I act on it. I buy a large can of cinnamon and sprinkle some on top of the ants' highway, and more on the ants' entrance tunnel. That's all I do: sprinkle cinnamon on the ants and bless them. The smell is heavenly.

In two days they are completely gone.

AND NOW A WORD FROM THE DEVIL

Every day, without fail, the newspaper I work for faithfully reports the projections of our joint human fear. Murder and mayhem, greed and cruelty, poverty and disease. I think that covers it—have I left anything out?

Good news ... well, that's another story. Good news is quietly cast aside as unfit to print. And really, it's easy to understand such a decision. Newspapers are printed for a human audience. That being so, why would a mind tilted enough to believe in separation be interested in joy?

Better to get on with the hot stuff—horror. Let us join together and be grim. Let us unite in progressive pain. As least it's a kind of bond, wouldn't you say?

No, you wouldn't say. If you're on the Path, and you are, you know what you have to do—you must publish your own daily newspaper. And that means getting your news (all of it) from the One Unimpeachable Source.

News of peace, news of safety, news of oneness. It's there, and it's waiting—your job is to collect it. And like all good reporters, you must do the job thoroughly. Bring Him all your questions, your doubts, your skepticism. Do not hold back. You must begin where you are, for there is simply no other starting point. Present any query, on any topic. There is only one answer to all questions, but you must hear It yourself to believe It.

So ask. What is the truth about this situation? Then sit still, and listen.

And listen, listen, listen, listen, listen.

Forget about the human skills and learning you have acquired. In this holy interview, write in no answers of your own; they will only taint or delay your moment of hearing.

Listen simply, the way water spills over rocks. Listen the way a bird sings, utterly without complications, following an urge from its heart.

Listen without fear. Love never hurts; hurt is not in its repertoire. Love will tell you something like this: pictures come and pictures go, but fear them not! Pictures are not the Truth.

And then ask Love this: "Mirror, mirror on the wall, who's the realest of them all?"

Now, listen to the answer: I Am.

In the Beginning Was the Word

What is a word? A symbol, yes. But is it more than that? Is a word larger than its letters?

And can a word possibly be a friend?

Oh, yes! In this infinite universe, a word is as large as we can stretch ourselves to receive it. Because words, like plants and pets and people, are alive. Or to put it more accurately, each has the potential to reveal All, if it is read by the soul rather than the eye. Taken as a series of letters, of course, words never deliver anything but a mechanical message. But let a cluster of holy words dwell in your heart—walk with them, sit with them, surrender to them—and sooner or later you will find their essence exploding open within your heart.

Koans are able to serve us in that way, and mantras. In centuries past, certain mystics would select one word, say, "God" or "Love" or "I," and wrap it capelike around their soul for years at a time. They would take this word with them forever—when they went walking, when they ate a meal, when they prayed, when they worked, when they visited a friend.

Yes, they carried it everywhere, but always, always keeping an ear bent toward it, waiting to hear it uncover its secrets. And over time, the Word would do just that. More than that, it would become so alive, so breathing, so full of Presence that the one wearing it would become completely immersed in Its Light.

So if you occasionally find yourself reading words and words without release (and don't we all do this sometimes?) try this: try taking just a few of them for a long, long walk. Sit with them; sink deep inside them and put aside any prior meanings and let the meaning come to you on its own. You will know it is there, because when it speaks, every cell in your body will leap up in recognition.

The Self within you already knows All, but you and I know nothing. So this practice of feeding deep on words of Truth is a daily calling, calling, calling to our Self. And holy words, the flowers of the alphabet, are often the bridge over which we inch slowly and silently back to our Self. And once there, once there we receive the gift that is beyond words, beyond price—moments of knowing.

Testing, Testing, 1, 2, 3

It's easy to believe in Goodness while we are drinking in the slow, velvet fragrance of a rose. There it is—beauty—all of our cells and senses confirm it.

Or when we are standing near a waterfall which is humming some divine melody and hurling cool love at us; droplets that look like liquid diamonds.

It's easy, too, to believe in the Goodness we see winking out from a loved one's eyes. Or celebrate the perfect beauty of a child's head-over-heels smile.

And who doesn't thank God for His grace when we are near a teacher whose presence is simply and wordlessly luminous?

I'm telling you something you already know: having faith during springtime is a piece of cake.

But now try remembering Divine Order is ever-present while the world is heaving and thrashing around us like a just-broken washing machine, or while *we* are heaving and thrashing around like a just-broken washing machine.

Try and believe in Peace then.

But you can! And yes, it requires the use of Silence.

This is our test. This is our daily test. Learning to shift our faith from an outer sense to an inner sense. Working towards the point where we can sink down inside our Self, trusting It to be as firm and steady and supportive as a field of fresh grass. Stepping into that indescribable space within which knows we are larger than littleness, greater than ego, huger than history, taller than time.

Then, then ... is when we begin putting less stock in the visible and more—much more—in the Can't-See-It-But-It's There.

The moment will come when we can see through the visible as easily and quickly as if it were gauze. And beyond the sheer, pale threads of this dream, Something Else will emerge, and emerge to stay. Something as real and sure and there for us as breathing.

But first ... *a few little tests*.

O HOLY NIGHT

Have you noticed how sacred stories seem to haunt us? Especially the one about Jesus. The story has such a familiar ring to it, and no wonder—the story of His birth is the story of someone else's birth too—yours, mine.

It's our story. The story of our wandering Hidden Heart, shining but poor, searching for a place to awaken. We trudge along, looking externally for help, but the world casually spurns us and pushes us away from the main tent. And why not? What possible value does a heart have next to the urgencies of this world? Wait a minute, though—there is this one, unremarkable room in the barn—we can use that.

And so begins our long, cold night of spiritual birth. In the story it is one night long; in our human life it is years. The baby Self is born, but Its surroundings are bleak and lonely. Only angels pay any attention. Plus a few oddball kinds. The rest of the world is seated in the warm, brightly lit dining room next door, having roast beef and ale.

In the story it is the innkeeper who carelessly shunts the Self off to the manger. In our life it is our own small self—the ego—which finds itself too saturated with pleasure, pain, and things material to take note of the birth cry of the Spirit.

So the story is a perfect roadmap for us, detailing all the dilemmas we experience as we move our attention away from body and things and stuff and into God. Our path unfolds, and yes, it is indeed filled with the very temptations the story has warned us about.

It's a perfect script, because it was written by a Mind that knew all. Day by day, our baby Self struggles forward on tiny feet towards a life of full love and awakening. Yet, sure enough, right in the next room there is that small separated self, busy doing everything it can to bring our attention back to world-stuff. And what an amazing bag of tricks it has to distract us with: scenes of poverty, scenes of wealth, scenes of tragedy, scenes of health, scenes of horror and suspense. Our false self uses them all, and time after time we find ourselves peering back into the world with excited eyes, captured again.

Now fast forward several years. You all know the happy ending. Despite distractions, insults, attacks, sabotage, annoyances and tears, our baby Self keeps growing and growing and growing and growing and growing. Moments of Peace appear out of nowhere. Sudden streaks of Light focus our sight. Pulses of Love shatter our darkness. And one day—one fine, holy, glorious, mind-stopping day, we discover that our small, sweet baby Self has quietly grown up and up and overcome human suffering. *Joy to the world!*

THE GREAT DISTRACTION

Here come the appearances, dancing across your horizon like clockwork. Aren't they something?

Battery's dead. Boss is grumpy. Kids have flu. Wars are waging. And look! There a hurricane—let's not even think about what that's doing. And naturally, a new disease has presented itself, a new incurable disease. Is there anything more? Well, there's your foot. It's tired. It aches.

But you're no fool; you know it's time to get still. Time to shift your focus onto the Real. That's what is called for.

But what's this? You don't want to. The pictures are compelling, too vivid to dismiss. And there's the rest of the world, busy chattering about it all like magpies; they want you to join in. So there you are, sneaking a bite of the carrot. Yes, even though it's made of stardust, you go for it. Have yourself a little carrot soup. Just a bite, mind you. It's so nice to belong!

Who knew? Who knew the world was simply one giant distraction? Full of seductions, keeping you safely away from the deep inner work you signed on to do.

Of course, there is one teeny tiny problem here. You find, after all, that the carrot isn't quite, well, satisfactory. Once you know a thing is faux, it becomes a lot harder to swallow. At first you chew out of habit, but as it turns out, you're not the same old you that you used to be. Are you? Inevitably you find yourself pulling away from the carrots and looking for a quiet tree to rest under. And you sit. You pause. You wrestle with the inescapable feelings of self-disgust. "How could I fall for that? Waste all that time? I'll never learn anything, ever."

Until it comes to you with a jolt: fencing with self-disgust is just one more distraction. One more barrier. One more closed door against God. And you drop it.

Now ... now you're ready.

Now you can let the troubled images drift away. Slowly, don't push. Open your mental fist and let them fall out. Easily. They have no staying power, really—stardust is stardust.

And here, here in the pool of Silence is the answer that's waiting for us time and time and time again. With no you left, there is no chaos left. All problems arise from the ripples in our mind, and when the ripples dissolve, nothing remains but the still, cool waters of our True Self.

CONFESSIONS OF A RECOVERING FORMAHOLIC

How did it all start? It was a silly thing, really. I dreamed I was born into a chunk of stuff. A baby body.

And then, out of nowhere, other chunks appeared—a soft, round body brought me food. A tall body swung me into the air. Things, delightful things, were dropped into my baby universe. So I continued on, using forms as my roadmap.

Here I found a sofa, there a gold chain, here a disease, there a new recipe for chili, here a job title, there a suffering, here a spring flower. These acquisitions all had two qualities in common— each seemed vividly real! And they were not enough.

Yes, yes, I admit it—surrounded by a dazzling green ficus plant, a ridiculously soft wing chair, a crystal glass humming with fine wine, some good friends, a stubbed toe, and a muffin, still ... still! ... I was not satisfied. Other forms beckoned; I followed. Surely peace would be at the bottom of this box! Well, then, maybe the next one.

How could I know then that this was an artificial self, living an artificial life?

Of course, the day came when, like everyone else, I had a first moment of sanity. For some it comes from a teacher. A book. Or maybe a dream. But come it will—the voice of Truth, informing us in one way or another about Real Life, vast and formless. And about You, also vast and formless. The awareness that changes how we see, and thus changes everything.

And following each realization of Truth comes the hard—I mean hard—work of living it, right here in our form-ridden world of good and evil. Moment by moment by moment. Appearance by appearance by appearance. Making mistakes— and forgiving them. Mis-perceiving. Mis-reacting. Mis-judging. Making problems real as mosquitoes. And when we do, starting all over again.

Yet, as other recovering formaholics have found, this life thing has gotten a whole lot simpler. I have only one job nowadays, only one— seeing past appearances into the Truth. And how do I do it? How do I do it?

One day at a time.

HICCUPS ON THE PATH

Questions float pollen-like in and out of our mind; here's one that's caused a sneeze or two in all of us.

If the One is alive in each of us, why, oh why, do we need a discipline? If It's right here, right now, why must we walk this tough, rigorous, no-wobbling path in search of the Unseen?

It's a universal question, as inevitable as the common cold and just as irksome. *Everyone* has raised this question once upon some time or other. In fact, if you haven't asked it, *you're not yet serious about the Work.*

We do a discipline; we walk the Path because the One is alive in us. It is alive, and It is all, but alas, something else seems to be present—our belief in a "you" and a "me." Our great, stuporous blind spot. And so we need the Path; it is a necessary tool, useful for noticing our considerable resistance to What Is. Before we can be free, we must become clear we are *operating as if* we are unfree. A discipline is our map out of the maze of separation we think we see before us.

And are we really caught in a maze? No. We already are What Is. But each of us has to discover that, just as an infant has to discover its own ten fingers. And before our knowledge is deep and sure, we must first look without judgment at our delusions. And make no mistake—it is the nature of the human mind to deny its wholeness, to prefer seeing itself as small, as limited, as fragile. Every human concept is dependent on the notion of limits for its validity. A great investment, then, has been made in smallness by our faux mind, and this mind will do anything to keep its investment intact.

So it's best to become at home with the fact that our "me" has no interest whatsoever in Oneness. It will resist What Is at every opportunity, in every unguarded moment. Get used to it! Here's a tip: don't take it personally. As fast as you can, get to the point where resistance ceases to alarm you. Let the faux mind resist as it will; your task, moment by moment, is to go into the Silence and listen to the Real.

Sooner or later we reach a moment when even our own resistance makes us chuckle. It is precisely at that point, Point Chuckle, when you know resistance has begun to lose its clout. And then, when you are able to see through the antics of the faux mind, when your "me" is as transparent as sunlit gauze, as motionless as grass on a hot day—guess what races in, alive and joyous, to fill up its place?

How the Ego Feels about that Darned Spiritual Path

Look, back in the days
when fudge was fudge,
and I was allowed to hold a grudge—
Things were simpler!
Things were swell!
We lived our life and went to hell.

None of this peace stuff,
none of this love.
Nobody asked what
we're fashioned of.
We drank and swore and gossiped, too.
And nobody said what we couldn't do.

But now all this goofy peace inside
is leavin' my brain completely fried!
I mean, if it's true that we're all One—
how on earth can I have any fun?

Because if I can't hate
the guy next door,
and trick my customers some more;
if I can't scream about the bills;
if I can't have a few cheap thrills;
if I can't fret about the war
and whine about an extra chore;
if I can't compare and judge and fuss—

how can I separate
them from us?

So listen up, friend—
here's the deal:
you don't meditate,
and I won't squeal.
See, I can't stand to sit and pray—
it puts a big crimp in my day!
I'll give you one second.
Maybe two.
But that's all I'll concede to you.
And if you spend longer when you sit,
I'm warning you—

I'll have a fit!
I won't put up with what you're doin'!
This spiritual stuff is
my road to ruin.

So if you start to go within,
I'll holler till your eyeballs spin!
Next time you try to be the Light—
I'm going out and start a fight!
And if that doesn't do the trick—
Hey—I'll get busy and make you sick.

Because
if there's one thing that I can't face,
it's finding out I'm
an empty _____.

CLIMBING OVER OUR WALL OF BELIEFS

Surely we cannot be closed against the boundless, numinous current of Love. Can we?

When we know It is the essence of all being, all movement, all stirring, all unfolding? When we know It is more real than rocks? Older than evermore? Fresher than wet spray? Sweeter than summer starlight? Closed against that? Us?

Yet we are; we are. Our sense of a linear world is itself a gate, shut tight against the One Presence. And yes, much of the ordinary common sense which is prized so highly is another. All movements, all concepts, all judgments stemming from the separated mind, a mind grasping desperately for love, all are gates blocking us from the very Substance we seek.

Believing you are in a room with another person is a gate.

Believing you are ill or in trouble is a gate.

Believing you are incredibly healthy is a gate.

Believing you are a physical entity is a gate.

Believing you know what to do is a gate.

Believing there is a human you at all is a gate.

Questioning those beliefs opens the latch.

Silence is the place in which we ask our unanswerable questions of the One who knows no second. Whatever words we use, prayer asks, *Who am I?*

And what actually happens when we are in the Presence? Do we see a mighty and merciful hand undoing our mistakes? No. If you pay close attention, you will notice we do not experience things being fixed. Something else happens. In the stillness of Love, we get a clear glimpse of the illusory nature of the gates which blind our vision.

And healing follows. For once seen with utter clarity, illusions vanish. Then, without any false concept barring its way, Love rushes forth. It may seem to do something wonderful, but the fact is, when we cease to bind ourselves with the cruel tourniquets we press upon our heart, there *is* nothing but wonders.

What else can there be? Love is an endless Wonder waiting moment by moment for a chance to sing Its song into your life. Be silent then, so that your heart can swing open wide.

And let out Love.

THE OBSTACLE

You have probably all heard the old story about an ardent Truth-seeker who wanted to see God more than anything else in this world. I'll tell it again anyway.

It seems that after years of getting nowhere in his spiritual pursuit, he learned by chance about a learned teacher who was able to see God.

Having heard that, nothing could stop him. He packed his bags at once and set out to find him. After many, many miles of difficult roads and treacherous weather, he finally reached the town where it was reported that the teacher lived.

The second after he set down his bags in the local hotel, he immediately set out for the teacher's home to request an interview. The teacher was extremely agreeable and told him to come back the next morning.

When finally the two of them were face to face, the teacher asked him, "What do you want?" And of course the student replied, "I want to see God."

"Well, you will never do that," said the teacher.

The student was devastated. "What?" he cried. "Never?"

"Never," insisted the teacher.

"But it is widely reported that *you* have seen God," said the student. "If you can do it, why can't I?"

Who told you that?" asked the teacher. "I myself have never seen God, not even once!"

The student was crushed. All his years of yearning had come to naught!

"But," continued the teacher in a kind voice, "there was a time when, like you, I wanted to do so."

"Yes?" asked the student. "What happened?"

"Well, after many fruitless attempts, I discovered that trying to see God is like the front of the head trying to see its own back. I couldn't do it."

"Yet everyone knows you swim in the Divine," said the student. "So tell me—what happened next?"

"Well, even though I was unable to see God, I still felt a burning desire to do just that," said the teacher. "So what I did was ask for the obstacle that was blocking my view to be removed. And it was. And that's that."

"And what was the obstacle?" asked the student. "Me," replied the teacher.

Marinate Before Serving

In algebra class, I was told by my exquisitely patient math teacher that in order to solve the equation $2x = 4$, I needed to divide 2 into 4. That guidance was repeated so often it finally burned itself into my skull. I could quote it at the drop of a hat.

But as for employing it — ah, that was a different story. I remained clumsy and inoperative around the more complicated algebra equations for a long time.

One day, however, I happened to sit down with an accredited algebra whiz, and in a weak moment I confessed my difficulties with the world of algebra. The whiz just shrugged and said, "Well, let's walk through one of the problems."

Sitting beside me, radiating some inner algebraic genius, he watched as I struggled through the equation inch by inch. When I wobbled, he asked a question designed to refer me back to the principles.

Finally, I succeeded in working the problem out — by myself. The whiz didn't do it for me, since he knew that would produce no learning. He simply nudged me away from wrong directions and prodded me into thinking it through. It worked.

Now here's the interesting part. After this stellar hands-on lesson, I found to my surprise that at long last the principles had actually integrated themselves into my thinking process. No longer did I sweat blindly, trying to work through a problem whose steps I did not understand. Solving became, finally, a viable exercise, because now I was steeped in the principles. The whiz had managed to marinate me in algebra.

And this path is no different, is it? Just so do we proceed in our adventure with spiritual principles. First we hear them, maybe even feel the sense of them. Next we study them, test them, consult with teachers, and practice working through the principles themselves, until we have proven them out and they have sunk deep, deep inside.

When, after trial and error and trial again, we have become thoroughly marinated, we find the principles are no longer abstract and inaccessible. Now they are an integral part of us. This is the point at which spiritual principles become truly useful to us, and to those around us. This is when they can (and do) impact our life.

So here is the moral to this story: become a food that nourishes all it touches—keep soaking yourself in God.

LEARNING TO LOVE YOU

Many years ago, as I began my spiritual practice (a rather haphazard one), I remember being flooded with a desire to see the sacred in every one I encountered. Seeing God everywhere was the endpoint of master teachers. They reach a place in which they are able to espy the Real Self in every being. So I wanted to get to that place as fast as possible.

I began to work at it—looking for the Light in this one and that one. It was an excellent practice for me to take up, and it still is. There have been many, many moments when I saw Something I would not ordinarily have seen, and felt a blessing flow out from that sight. As time passed, however, and what seemed like an inordinate amount of tough lessons came my way, I began to get an inkling that there was something essential missing from my practice.

What occurred to me was that in my earnest search for the Sacred in all beings there was one being I was grievously neglecting. Me.

Now, I know full well that "me" is the element we are wanting to drop away. "Me" is our prison, and on the path we are working for a release. But the interesting thing about freedom is that we earn our way into that state through love, and a primary focus for our love must be the "me" we so much do not like.

You've heard that before, and so had I. But it had not yet *dawned on me*. Then, at a certain point of awareness, I began to feel the truth of it from my heart. I cannot authentically love another person until I have learned to respect and honor myself. And what does that entail? It means forgiving myself for my mistakes. It means noticing my flaws and attachments with a loving eye. It means learning to say no when I feel a no in my heart. And learning to say yes when yes comes from deep within. It means learning to honor my intuitions, whether they are popular or not. It means being patient with the parts of me that are still asleep. It means rejoicing over the fact that Grace can flow through this odd, flawed little instrument in which I appear to be housed.

In the world of Spirit, you are loved mightily. Please, don't forget to love you, too.

How else can we all awaken?

THE VISITOR

With me, it happens in a split second and for no discernible reason. Out of nowhere, I find myself overcome with a wash of gratitude for everything, everyone. And each time, I know that whatever the sudden waterfall of thanks is, it certainly does not come from me, the little i who trundles along keeping a watchful eye out for sand traps and bee stings. No, it comes from a place much deeper—from my Self—and accordingly It seems both odd and familiar at the same time. Although I walk around as ordinary as ever, this unseen Visitor rushes forward with quiet feet and tumbles over everything I meet.

As a result, I find myself staring with gratitude at the chair, the radio, at a cup of tea in my hand. Feeling grateful for the sun, reaching inside to paint itself across the living room floor. And grateful for the windows that permit me to watch elm leaves dancing in the sky. Grateful for an ant, alive and purposeful, hurrying along a baseboard to complete its chores. Grateful for the familiar face of a neighbor, jogging casually along my street. Grateful for an unexpected idea which burst into my morning out of the blue. Grateful for an old jacket, which has served me kindly and gently for so many years. Grateful for breath, grateful for flowers, grateful for life.

But that isn't all. I tell you, this unearthly gratitude is so expansive, so ocean-wide and un-blinking, that it even embraces things that would normally be trigger points—like bills, like burnt toast, like a sore back.

And after some time it passes, this immense blessing, as quietly as it comes. For a while I just sit there, looking around the apartment with a sense of emptiness, wanting it back again—this formless, timeless, healing, heart-filling taste of eternal Love.

And of course, It has never left. It is I, with my subtle attachments to this world, who keep It at a distance.

But here is my wish for all of us this year: may the Visitor come to our door, and find us ready.

GUIDANCE 101

"How can you tell the difference between divine advice and your own thoughts?" someone asked recently. She was in a quandary and unsure about what she was hearing.

She is not alone. Her query is one probably all of us have made at times, because when a question arises, indeed it is not always clear which part of us is doing the answering.

Many people I know, including myself, test responses to problems by first giving them a field of time in which to rest. If they're ego-based, they wobble. If they hold, they're real.

Often, when I'm not completely sure about what direction I need to take, I simply ask again. One thing is clear: advice from Within is sourced from Peace and has a beneficent color to it, whereas advice from the small mind is invariably tainted with small concerns.

Particularly open to question are actions that follow an upset. If someone has annoyed me or hurt me in some way, I must be doubly careful before responding. If I reply from anger—which is the voice of fear—I am clearly going to worsen the situation.

On the other hand, if I pause and set my attention on receiving guidance from the voice of

Love, I can trust that whatever response I am led to make, it will be pointed toward healing.

I remember one particular instance when I was convinced that a certain company was treating me unfairly. The voice of fear was flooding me with unhappy thoughts, and, not surprisingly, I was deeply tempted to respond from that place, citing my rights in a flurry of indignation. Sorely tempted.

But I decided to wait and pray about the matter first. And I did—prayed for several days, asking for guidance, asking to see the situation in a holier way. Each day I felt calmer, until finally I was able to forgive the company, forgive the people involved, and forgive what I had seen as an injustice. Eventually a series of corrective steps came to me, and I took them in an unhurried and unruffled way. By the time I was finished, I discovered I no longer had any investment in the outcome. The issue seemed small and unimportant.

In this particular case, the result was a new and happier adjustment in my behalf from the company. Now, I know from experience that not all prayer work yields improved external results; but I do know that it always leads to a change within us, and that, it seems to me, is a more than sufficient reward. Because that reward is peace, which is priceless. It's the water of life we're all searching for.

To be able to remain undampened, unsoured, unsquashed, no matter what nonsense is going on around us or within us, is the secret to happiness.

And only a divine hand can point out the way to us.

SOME OF MY BEST FRIENDS
ARE ENEMIES

We clean out our closets, our attic, our garage, our desk drawers, and we feel suddenly lighter. More free. The air smells (is this possible?) sweeter.

It's possible. Simple is pure. Simple is clean. With less load around our human neck, our step does indeed lighten. Simple is easier to live with.

And that's not all. If a clean closet can float the heart, imagine how free we feel when we drop our deeper burdens, opinions, points of view, judgments, labels, belief upon belief upon belief, and above all, wanting to be right about them.

I remember one time when I felt sure a friend had made an error in judgment. You may have thought so too, had you been there. But very possibly, you being wiser than I, you would have then blessed it and dropped it out of sight. Not me—I held onto it.

The notion of this "mistake" nestled deep in my mind like a prickly pear. For days, it itched and tickled. I scratched and it got worse; began to fester. By the end of the week I was a haunted house. With each irritated thought I shrank smaller and smaller, until finally I was merely a dark human dot on the map of time and space. A black hole, collapsing inward from the weight of my somethingness.

But then! Misery itself startled me into silence. What was I doing here, I asked, trapped in so small and suffocating a space? And while I was pausing, angels arrived with reminders from within.

So I stayed put, leaving all opinions well behind, and bathed for a long while in the Silence. When I emerged again, the landscape looked very different. For one thing, the error which had previously loomed so large and grim, now looked like a small fleck on the horizon—a puny thing, worth scarcely more than a smile.

But a not small thing was now surrounding it—miles and miles and miles of clear, untroubled landscape; the space we call holy, because it is unmarred by human beliefs of any kind. Simple peace.

So I returned to my day bringing nothing. My notions, my rightness, my perceptions—all abandoned. I no longer recall the details of the day's events; the only thing I can remember is that all day long I felt like a feather. All day long it glowed.

WASHING OUR WINDOWS

Awareness is a lot like a colorless stain remover, spreading slowly, slowly across the threads of our ordinary mindset until it has seeped into everything, dissolving old patterns and cleansing off useless spots.

Why doesn't it happen faster? There's no mystery to that. It's because we resist waking up. Our habitual thoughts are comfortable as old shoes, and part of us wants to keep on wearing them.

I want to be free, but I like some of my cages, too. And I only know one way to make headway with the cages—by paying them very close attention.

Think about it. There are so many things we are willing to study closely: birds or flowers or stars or pets or how to grow vegetables. We are willing to pay enormous attention to our profession, getting the subtleties of it, learning its tricks. We will study someone we care about with infinite patience, looking for clues, looking for insights into their own unique wiring.

But when it comes to watching the workings of our own mind, often we bow out; don't want to be bothered. It seems too much effort. Some of us aren't even certain that the mind has workings that are observable.

And yet this mind is our window to the world, the opening through which we perceive all that we perceive. How can we possibly awaken to a larger, more luminous view without first beginning to question the authenticity of our smaller, denser window?

Maybe it is possible to see Light without checking out the way we tend to "see through a glass darkly." In my case, this examination has been a necessary (even crucial) process, without which, I am certain, I would still be caught up in the lens of darkness day in and day out.

And, for me, the secret of watching has been to do it without judgment. (How often have we heard that?) Neutral examination is hard to do, because our mind is an automatic judgment machine, printing out yea or nay like a computer. So it takes some practice to watch the mind patiently and intently without voting on its contents.

Here's why it makes sense to go through this often tedious and burdensome effort: once we begin to see (and I mean *truly see*) how the mind thinks, how it searches out chaos and trouble, how it jumps to align itself with separation, how it hugs pain, we begin to be free of its conclusions. To the extent that I grasp deeply and finally that I am being conned by my own thoughts, my own reactions, I am free of the next con game.

To the extent that I have *not* caught on to the spurious motions of my mind, I am simply a fresh tuna ready for the next hook.

So pay attention.

IN GOD I TRUST — *SOMETIMES*

This probably never happens to you. But it does to me.

Every now and then I have what we humans are fond of calling a bad day. It's cold, it's wet, an assignment is overdue. Oh—and my hair is a mess. Does it stop there? Don't be silly. Next thing I know I encounter a snapdragon waitress—*really* rude, *really* insensitive. (You would have thought so, too.) And what happens? My eyes narrow. My lips tighten. I begin a slow, inward slide into dislike. Perfectly reasonable, right? Well ...

Take a look at it for a moment. What am I trusting in this instance? I am trusting that the waitress' bad mood is who she is. I am trusting that my unkind response to her is justified, because who I am is an insulted party. I am seeing nothing and putting all of my money on it. Or, as they say in Brooklyn, "I'm taking it poissonally."

Is she a snapdragon? Am I an insulted party? Hardly. She and I are both creatures trapped in a dark thought. And then putting all of our faith in that dark thought. In pain I trust.

And where is God while this is going on? To be blunt about it, He's been shut out. He is the Light which I have temporarily shelved for the pleasure of nursing a hurt. You mean someone who has been practicing for years could do something this stupid? You bet. *And will again.*

Here's where the practice helps, immeasurably. It doesn't take me very long to spot the quick-sand into which I have sunk and to take a hard look at my misplaced trust. *There I go again, trusting in appearances!*

So I catch my mistake as it's cooking and pull it straight off the griddle. And I remind myself of the truth. I can't walk in peace if I place God in the glove compartment and drive on without Him. There is a certain point on the path where we realize—*deeply*—that it is imperative we carry Him with us everywhere. In the kitchen, in the office, on the highway, in the restaurant, in the mall. Because who else is there to trust? More to the point—who else is there?

Years ago I realized I must undo my habit of expecting the world to behave and feeling crushed when it does not. I came to see I must walk around in the world and yet—at the same time—leave it alone. A dream is a dream is a dream. My task was to hold fast to His love. And not just hold fast to It, but use It daily, hourly, as my Seeing-Eye dog while wandering the labyrinth of the marketplace. Only His eye can catch the curbs I may otherwise trip on.

And that is the core of my practice. Is it perfect? If it were, I wouldn't have any waitress stories to tell you. But I'm working on it. I'm working on it. And one day, possibly they'll be able to say about me what they say about the ones up ahead on the road:

"In God she trusts. Period."

ACCEPTANCE

So many of the deepest treasures in this world are hidden.

The big, splashy, overt kind we already know about. Warm, spring rain whispering across your face as you walk through the woods; the scrunch and rub of fresh grass under your toes. Rolling in the snow, safely protected by scarf bundlings and mittenry. Hearing Mozart. Hearing Sinatra. Hearing the voice of an old friend you've been missing for months. A great, taut, well-written movie. Good hot tea. Good hot coffee. Sitting with friends near a fireplace blazing with life. Reading a great book. A discreet taste of gourmet chocolate. A child laughing. You laughing. Anyone laughing.

These are our obvious treasures.

To get to the secret ones, you have to move very carefully and quietly, preferably with your shoes off. You must be looking without haste, without greed, without anxiety. You must have made at least a primitive alliance with meditation. Then, as the poets say, the world can unfold itself at your feet.

The tick of a clock on your shelf can start sounding like the heartbeat of God.

Washing a cup can become art. Watching its stains slide away with the soap is as thrilling as a stab of lightning.

Everything—floors, ceiling, windows, furniture, seem to shift gently into benign objects which are here to help.

Listening grows multi-dimensional. Someone brags, and you can hear the pleading underneath the boast; it moves you to enormous tenderness. Another giggles, and you can hear each note of laughter fly through the air like birds on holiday.

New hints, new clues appear in unexpected places. Exit signs on the subway read like messages about oneness. A pet, always your delight, is now even more—your teacher. You open the kitchen cupboard and withdraw a can of food; instantly you understand how the can and the peas within it are related. Small revelations, per-haps, but thunderous in their impact.

This network of insights occurs because you are in a state of extreme openness, one in which your eye can see far deeper into each object than it normally does, and your mind now floods you with awarenesses about the nature of life. Some call it inner guidance.

It's an extraordinary discovery, really—finding the exquisite intelligence that lies within our own mind, waiting for permission to emerge. In the beginning, it's hard to fathom that magic can occur from withdrawing attention from the outside world, because we are so used to seeking outside ourselves for drama and movement and color. But hard to fathom or not, the fact is that the universe within us is far, far larger and richer than the universe without.

And becoming still is what opens the door.

BLUE SKY

Here is the blue sky
enduring beyond all borders,
capable of enclosing
myriad elements:
clouds, heat, rain, tears, hailstones,
stars, light, planets, bursting comets,
infinite colors, mist.

Here is the blue sky
with its unreachable ceiling,
an open doorway to always;
the screen upon which
all passions play,
all songs and sorrows
emerge and dissolve,
home to soaring birds.
and You,
You are the blue sky.

EVIDENCE OF GOD

I saw something recently
that sent a sudden whisper
into my soul
about the amazingness
and sheer generosity of God.

I had a chance to witness
a pair of healing hands,
side by side, hands without pretense,
designed by an unerring Architect,
shaped by living and learning
and used by a loving spirit
with a vast consciousness of good.
These hands were, quite simply,
a work of art;
there was no mistaking
–not even for a moment–
Who had created them.

And I can't help but think
when I see something as transfusing
as a strong, capable,
incandescent hand,
one that seems unusually informed
by Divine Light,
that there is never a need
to doubt the grace of God
or the fact that Divine Order

has a firm hold on things,
and always will.
Yes, always will,
no matter what chaos appears
to hold sway over our lives
at this moment.

For me, seeing those hands
offered a split-second
reminder of heaven.
A brief taste of God's
divine and splendid magic.
Hasn't such a reminder come
once or twice to you?
I'm sure it has.

Because right here
in our dusty, flawed little world
there's a million—no—a trillion
living and holy wonders;
all of them whisper of God,
some even sing of Him.
And I fervently hope
you encounter one today.

I hope you see a talking tree,
or a simple weed dancing,
or a cloud shaped like a face,
or a smile that speaks of heaven.

As for me, what I saw was
one pair of healing hands,

close up and beautiful.
And, really, that's all it takes
for my heart to know
that He is Real
and He is Here
and He is Love.

THE FOUNTAIN

I was outside
watching a fountain at work.
Well, maybe work
is the wrong word.
It was laughing, hurling itself
wrong-side up into the sky,
then splashing down again
on the back of gravity.

A small child wandered by,
waving a deliciously bent stick
which he heaved into the froth.

Instantly the water wrapped
itself lightly around that stick,
kept on moving,
curling, jumping, singing
without missing a beat.

Then the child found a stone,
and he threw that, too,
into the fountain,
using all his eight-year-old strength.
As soon as the stone fell splat
into the quick shivering streams,
they kindly made way for it,
not even pausing to say ouch.

If that stone had landed
on my slow dense body,

I would own a purple bruise now
as evidence that my cells
are collective soldiers,
trained to resist blows.

But not water. Not water.
Water simply splices open its arms
and lets everything tumble by
in a wash of forgiveness—
rocks, branches, people, fish,
even soda cans,
and keeps rushing onward
as if life were all about joy
and that's that.

Don't bother trying to stop me,
says each little water drop,
I'm too busy dancing.

Divine Love is like that.
Rivers of joy endlessly
flowing, forgiving, nurturing,
laughing, whispering, healing,
breathing love.

Holy One,
let me be
your vehicle
for That.

GIVING THANKS

MY THANK YOU SONG

I slide pale butter on a slice of crisp, seeded toast, and once again the familiar, hot, nourishing taste is a treasure for my tongue. Thank You.

Walking to the store on a slow balmy day, a sudden spray from heaven begins tickling my cheeks, my hair, my hands, my face, my feet. It moistens my morale. I think, "This is gentleness raised to the level of art." Thank You.

A friend calls, and for one quick moment we laugh wildly about something inordinately silly, briefly escaping the wash of mundanity that glues one day to the next. Thank You.

Out of nowhere a morning arrives when I find no pain, no stiffness, no tedious insults visiting the cells in my body. Painlessness is freedom. Thank You.

Pursuing the elusive fragrance of peace, I put on one of my cherished Bach CDs, and let my divine friend Johann Sebastian remind me that the music of heaven is always only a fingertip away. Thank you.

I stumble upon a delicious, stunningly irreverent movie and sink deep inside its imaginary universe in spellbound fascination. Thank You.

A dazzling six a.m. sun thrusts its life and energy into my window, and I watch it light up the world with a cup of hot, perfect coffee in my hand. Thank You.

Working on my keyboard, the image of a face I love floats into my consciousness. I close my eyes and watch it for a while, recalling how amazingly the hair, brow, cheeks, eyes, and mouth all unite together in one unforgettable concert. Thank You.

I spot one fallen green leaf on the street and place it in my palm, marveling at the intricacy, purpose, and elegance of its design. *Nobody* does it better. Thank You.

And thank You, too, for the unfathomable wonders that still await.

HELLO TO YOU

Hello to You,
and Your luminous dance,
pouring unseen heart into our dream
without pause.

Hello to Your awesome hands
guiding invisible threads into place
bit by inimitable bit,
until suddenly, wild patterns explode,
lighting up the corridors of thought,
opening new doors to heaven,
inching us closer to You.

Don't think we're not grateful.

HOW DO WE GROW?

If you can accept the concept
that we are here to remember
we are divine
—despite all contrary evidence—
and that, just for now, we are
briefly cast in these human bodies;
if you can enfold that into your heart—

then do not quarrel
with the lessons sent.

Yes, you will be surprised
a thousand and one times
in a thousand and one ways,
and your teachers will come
in a thousand and one disguises.

But if you follow the thread
in front of you at any moment,
you will discover
it is always placed there
as a tool for awakening
into unending Light,
so that you can have a taste
of borderless Love.
And following that,
serve it to others.

There is simply
no other agenda in heaven.
There is no other plan
in God's heart.

JOINING

Oneness is a substance,
like fine wine;
and it is harvested in the mind.
You start with an intention
to join with the sacred place
in another being.
And then you just do it.

It can be someone near
or someone miles away.
Either will do.
Do you think God knows what distance is?
Of course not. God's eye contains
all of the universe in one sweep.
Many of you ask,
But how can I join with someone
who has injured me?
You think, if I join silently with this one,
am I not asking to be hurt again?
Put this thought away forever.
When a flower offers pollen to a bee
does it underwrite the bee's sting?
Hardly! What the flower's gift does
is empower new honey.

Risk your beliefs
about how this world works.
Join with someone in your heart.
Doing this one thing
invites heaven into your life
and makes the journey home lighter
and less arduous
for every living being.

It's not a hard thing to do, joining,
once you see it's the Truth.
You are the green in my blue.
I am the blue in your green.
And God uses us
to paint His rainbow.

LOYALTY

I know someone you don't always believe in; someone who deserves it. Someone with built-in radiance, someone rarer than four-leaf clovers and twice as amazing. Someone you have abandoned a thousand times during dark days, despite all the evidence of great value issuing from the heart of this creature.

That someone is you.

Of course you are faithful during the good times; I know that. It's in the dark times when you need to show support; and these are the times you are most apt to take off running, labeling yourself a muddler or a goofball or worse.

This abandonment in crisis is a mistake; it's precisely when situations have hard rocks inside them that your best efforts are needed. Now is the time you need to remind yourself of your infinite capacities and hidden colors. Now is the time to believe in yourself and what you can see, what you can do, what you can know. If at some moment you are completely caught up in self-dislike, you may have to borrow a friend to remind yourself of your value. Do it. That's what friends are for.

Next week, you can return the favor.

This is a generous university in which we are enrolled; mistakes are allowed. You are even allowed to flunk courses; we all do. What happens, very simply, is that you take those courses over again, this time watching out for the potholes. Eventually you pass; we all do.

In the meantime, be kindhearted about your frailties and failures and stumblings. We're all like children in one respect: we respond more to kindness than to abrasion. When you drop a brick on your own feet, say ouch and learn to smile about it. Or at least grin a little.

The reason it pays to remain loyal to your self is that your self is dazzling. No matter what things look like at 3 a.m. in the morning, there is much, much more to you than your history and your container; more than you can see, more than you can even guess about.

The human beings who inspire us, who make us remember them from one century to the next, are invariably the ones who treated themselves gently. They are the ones who caught hold of their inner spirit and let it swing them into giant arcs of movement, imagination and faith. By remaining loyal to their inner Self they give that Self the power to take them for a wild and riveting ride.

We don't remember the ones who ignored their Self and spent their time muttering.

So on the day when rain jumps out of the sky and splatter spoils your day and you slip into a funk—be loyal.

You're worth it.

MOTHER TERESA

Once
Mother Teresa was asked
how she could continue
day after day after day,
visiting the terminally ill:
feeding them, touching them,
wiping their brows,
giving them comfort
as they lay dying.

And she said,
"It's not hard,
because in each one
I see the face of Christ
in one of His more
distressing disguises."

And that
is Mother's teaching:
to urge us to see
the face of Christ
in each of His
numerous disguises
wherever we go.

Her plea was
that we look for holiness
not just in those
who are ill or hungry
or in obvious pain,
but in all the others, too.
I mean those
who are suffering
from spiritual despair
or emotional imprisonments
which block their aliveness;
restrict their freedom
and wall them off
from limitless joy
and self-realization.

These beings too,
need our Silent Love,
for their pain is just as deep.

That is
Mother Teresa's message
about spiritual healing.
And the truth is,
there are countless numbers
of brothers and sisters
who urgently need
our blessing.

You don't have to go far
to find them.
They're right beside you at work;
they drive next to you
on the freeway;
they shop with you at
the grocery store.

In fact,
you can probably
find someone
you need to bless
right in your own mirror.

No Color

Once I sat with a teacher who had so dissolved her discrete self that there was nothing left except Everything.

Sitting with her was a lesson in fulfillment. We were having lunch, and our topics of discussion were as ordinary as they can get. And yet, due to the absence of history and programming on her plate, light danced on the table everywhere.

That was an enormous lunch.

I knew right then that this was the way, this was the work. To become transparent, to become a being of no color. To become walking food.

Of course, evolving into a human transparency is a slow process, one that occurs at a deep level of the heart. And no, it doesn't mean that our surface self loses all opinions or all sense of savvy about living.

It just means that we reverse our priorities. Where before, smartness was our main card, our chief ace in the hole, and the soul a buried treasure, now there is a switch. Now our opinions and history are like small, harmless flowers in a buttonhole, and the self is the main garment.

Walk around with the Self unhidden and you are walking around with heaven's blood coursing through your veins—and watering all life forms around you.

You do have to give up a few things to do this. You have to give up thinking small. You have to give up thinking you are helpless. You have to give up thinking you are something of any kind. You just kind of wear your personality over your shoulder like a loose sweater and stop taking it so seriously.

It takes great love to accomplish this. You must love the little self you carry along with you. Love it, honor it, humor it—but never let it drive the car.

Can we actually arrive at this point?

Oh, yes. We can be there, we can walk there, we can do there. But only after we stop viewing it as impossible.

If Brother Lawrence could reach the point where he actually loved washing his pots and pans for God (and he did), you and I can love our pesky little mindsets. Show some compassion! Eventually they melt away.

Eventually they melt away, and you can still enjoy a crisp, green, fresh Caesar salad, sip fine wine, and sing your favorite rock and roll tune in the shower. But underneath these discrete preferences you will notice the hum of no color, no thing, no two.

The hum of heaven.

ONE HAND CLAPPING

To be seared by the fire of God, as many of us are, is to be placed on the road to freedom.

Of course, at first it doesn't feel much like freedom. Those who find spiritual pacemakers lodged in their hearts are immediately challenged to learn how to view life inside out—and whatever our history, that is not an easy task. As human beings, we are taught to think of ourselves as the body and personality we wear. Discarding this notion often feels like we are being asked to pull off one of our own fingernails. And without anesthetic. So much for easy transformations.

"Get ready for some hard work" ought to be the motto for those embarking on the spiritual path. If you haven't discovered this yet, you haven't caught on to the nature of Divine Guidance. Love is all there is, oh yes, but that doesn't mean waking up is a matter of sending out more Hallmark cards and placing a bouquet of scented candles over the fireplace. (Although there is nothing wrong with cards and candles!) It means discovering how relentlessly and persistently we avoid Being.

Noticing stuff like that can make your eyes spin.

On the spiritual path we learn that our body, our history, and our personality are not who we are. We learn that we are Spirit, and that Spirit is an anathema to our everyday ego. Wars have been fought over the difference in viewpoint between these two sets of lenses. One viewpoint is real, one is not—but never mind that, wars are fought anyway.

Our ego's investment in remaining small, finite, scarcity-driven and headed for death is larger than the national debt. We are trained to be small, and small is comfortable, and comfortable is—well, let's just say that to the ego it is a plus.

So never ask why it is hard to meditate (a word which signifies pointing your attention toward God and away from out there); far better to ask what amazing Higher Source drives you to attempt being silent and listening in the first place.

It's that God stuff again, eternal pulses of Inner Light nudging you into remembering who you are. And nudging ... and nudging.

And so, who are you?

There's no way to say it perfectly, which means there are infinite ways to say it imperfectly. You are Spirit. And what is that?

Discovering what we are is why we are here. Somewhere inside we already know what that is, but the message hasn't sunk into our body-mind yet. We are water drops searching for the answer to, "What is water?" It takes time to uncover answers that are this difficult.

So we proceed. We seek. We study. We pray. We ask the right questions. Take the koan, "What is the sound of one hand clapping?" This is one of those famous Zen mind-benders designed to pop open the mind of seekers for a split second so that Vision can enter and saturate the awareness.

That's its purpose. Eight words—one goal.

And here you are, imagining one hand held up before you. It appears to have five separate fingers—all different, all useful, all fingers. Does each finger dream it is a separate entity? Because that is what we, a collage of human beings, think about ourselves—that we are separate entities scrambling for placement in an uncaring world.

We are finger one versus finger two versus finger three. Finger one is better off. After all, it is carrying a substantial and costly ring. Finger two has no ring, a child of poverty. Finger three and four have scars, inscribed since childhood, but they have overcome this obstacle to become useful and respected citizens. (Clearly, they deserve an award.) Finger five has power and leverage because it was born a thumb. All other fingers are jealous of thumb's high rank, but are too polite to let on and are completely powerless to change the situation anyway. Finger five likes being the thumb but complains privately that it has to do most of the work. See? Nothing's perfect in fingerland.

Trapped by separation.

That's us—simultaneously trapped and entranced by thoughts of separation. Entranced, because there is the dazzling possibility that maybe we, too, can someday become a thumb and rule the universe. Trapped, because once we are voted thumb, we discover the territory is limited and the rewards picayune.

You can see the problem: remain a material finger, even a thumb, and your world is still small enough to pinch.

So we turn back to the world of Divine Guidance. We ask ourselves again: what is the sound of one hand clapping? Our body-mind replies that the question is absurd, impossible, ridiculous. And so, from a separate finger's point of view, it is.

But drop the question—bang! and keep very, very still, not-knowing, and something else emerges out of the blue—vision.

What is the sound of one hand clapping? You are.

You are not one finger, but all fingers—and the palm out of which they grow, and the wrist which underwrites the palm, and the arm which holds the wrist, and the shoulder which sponsors the arm, and the body which claims the shoulder, and the breath which informs the body, and the feet which carry the breath, and the earth which supports the feet, and the space which surrounds the earth, and the life which inhabits all space—

and the luminous, vibrant, boundless, breathing, intelligent God from which all spring.

You are Spirit. You are the life, the light, the truth, the universe. You are the One, dreaming Itself the many. Why are you doing that? It doesn't matter. Only one fact is important.

You are the sound of one hand clapping.

RARE MOMENTS

Rowing through
an ordinary week
with its infinite capacity
for random nonsense
and grittiness and glum weather,
what strikes me is not so much
the wear of everyday sticks and stones,
but rather the fact that one
clear, awesome moment of Light
can plunk itself into our day
quite without warning
and catch us by surprise.

For instance, perhaps you are
simply standing around
chatting with a fellow human being,
and the next thing you know
— in one split second —
the person before you
turns out to be something more:
an angel in disguise.
In that moment, thinking stops.
A quick flash of divinity —
and there is no rhyme or reason for it;

it's just how things
sometimes arrange themselves.
Sudden starlight arrowing into the day
unheralded and unannounced.

After a glimpse like that,
all you can do
is be silent and say thanks.
Experiences of that sort are
simply too large to speak about.
You know what I mean—
the wind can't fit into a teacup.

So there it is. There you are.
And when I look back at the week,
rolling it out quick like a carpet,
that's what I see, clear and stark
and sharper than everything else—
the encounter with a being of Light.
What else is worth remembering?

So I guess the rest of the week
can do whatever it wants to do—
I had the Moment.

Thank You, Lord.

Rough Spots

Yes, there are places along the way
that feel cold, with rough edges;
places that seem alien or shrill,
unsoftened by sunlight.
Places poorly lit by kindness
or grievously empty of grace.

And it's OK to not like the tough spots;
don't think every moment
will be incandescent. It won't.
It's all part of the journey.
The task is to walk on anyway,
disliking the chill, but still walking,
still looking upward.
Accepting the arduous
with quiet flexibility
is the mark of heroes.

Something inside us knows
The Light is there even when
Our eyes cannot glimpse It;
Something inside us knows
our destiny is joy,
and nothing else.

Every stretch of the road,
grim or glorious,
has its own irreducible purpose.
It's a test; it's a test.

The Light is asking,
Can you see Me when I've ducked
around the corner?
Can you hear Me whisper
when you are bound by rocks?
If you can do that—
if you will use your soul
as an internal compass
to navigate through bitter waters,
you win it all.

Because the fact is,
Love never abandons us.
How can It? You are
Its heart, Its hands, Its voice.
However daunting the landscape,
you are embraced forever,
because Love is a fierce thing,
wildly creative, eternally right.
And Love will bring you Home.

SANDCASTLES

I was taking a walk along the beach.

It was a do-nothing walk, the kind where you take long strides into nowhere, carrying hot beads of sand under your toes. At some point I began watching the water sweep up over the sand. The wet waves left marvelous and intricate pictures each time they surged onto the shore—living art. I noticed the images could resemble anything: angels, skylines, puppy dogs, machine guns, planets—almost every form there is lay briefly on the face of the sand.

Yet just a heartbeat later, the water quietly withdrew, and the pictures dissolved into nothing. Then, once again, the sea would heave itself up into a huge living wave and spill itself over the beach, causing a new collection of profiles to form on the broad sand canvas.

I thought, isn't that how it is in our everyday human life? Minute by minute, images wash up on the shore of our mind; then—whoosh!—they are gone, and a barrage of new ones rush in to take their place.

Just like the pictures made by the sea, they are not permanent. They seem real, though, if we stare at them. And that's the catch—it's our habit to stare at external images. Yet the more we do, the more we become lost in their outlines. We stare, we memorize, we step inside them—and before we know it, our perspective shrinks from beholder to participant to victim. Having lost our broader overview, we seem—once again—to be at the mercy of the images that populate this world.

So enthralled are we with pictures and pictures of pictures that we neglect to pay attention to the Force out of which they arise.

Which is why so many teachers have cautioned us over and over and over again to with-draw our faith in appearances. Not just the awful images— the lovely ones, too. Because, they tell us, as long as we hold any image as valuable, we will miss the point: images are not real. They are images. We can never realize that distressing forms are nothing as long as we are insisting that the pretty ones have substance.

If, as we walk along the beach, we become over-enthralled with one of the designs—"Oh, what a beautiful castle!"—we cannot escape our inevitable disappointment when it melts back into the sea. More importantly, we lose our spiritual perspective, our ability to stand back and *see*.

The fact is, only when we surrender to a wider view and allow ourselves to absorb the entire shoreline—the endless process of images appearing and disappearing before us—only then can we experience the Divine Foundation that underlies all images. Only then can we discern that the pictures, however vivid, have no power or effect at all upon the Eternal Shore.

Which is why it is such a perfect place to rest our feet.

SIGNALS

In heaven, it is kindness
that evokes the most music.
Each small benevolence we do
sends a swift flash of Light
into the ethers beyond us.
When God peers
into the faint, darkened mist
that blankets this earthly dream,
that is all He can see:
dazzling pulses of Light.
Nothing more.

You doubt me? It's true.
Like a skilled and devoted gardener,
He watches each plant, each leaf,
each tender life form
for signs of awakening.
Light is how He measures growth.
And all kindnesses, large or small,
create the same telltale light burst.

Raise funds to heal a disease,
and that is indeed a kindness.
Carry a helpless soul
from a burning building,
and that is kindness, too.
Light will arise from it.

But guess what?
Quieter stuff also streaks
heavenward with the same
intense laser brightness.

I once knew someone who sat
at the bedside of a stranger
for four hours straight
in order to offer comfort.
Why did she do it? Compassion.
Now, there's a streak of Light.

I saw another person
run two blocks, panting hard,
to return a wallet to someone
who had dropped it on the street.
Why did he do it? Compassion.
Light leapt on that day.

As a matter of fact,
I've witnessed kindness even closer.
I have a friend who has a way
of making me feel deeply special
even though, in truth, I play
only a miniscule role in his life.
Why does he do it? Compassion.
Another wild burst of Light.

And like any passionate gardener
watching over his beloved plants,
God sees each flash, nods,
and takes loving note.

THE SMILE

She wore a certain smile; at first glance it was no different than any other smile, yet there was a quality to it that was miles away from most. It had radiance.

And it had depth. This smile spoke volumes about the heart that informed it. It was no "Hello, let's get it over with" smile, or a "smiling because it's appropriate" gesture. This smile was an intentional blessing: body, mind, and spirit were all participants in the event. How did it feel to receive it? Like being washed in gold.

So it was the kind of smile that blesses your day. You walk away knowing there is beneficence present and you've been lucky enough to encounter it. More than that, it was a potent reminder to move out of robot mode and be authentic.

It was a smile with some Aum in it.

It's so simple, really, to make a difference. Be here now, as Ram Dass so often told us. Be here now, and things start taking care of themselves. Instead of living from the skin out, try operating out of stillness; let your spiritual guidance arise from within and ease out of your being like a pale breeze carrying honey. Personal growth by way of grace.

Or try something even more subtle than a smile—a silent blessing. I remember some years ago attending a business meeting in which discord was high on the agenda. Communications were shooting out like bullets and scattering willy-nilly around the room. Industrial strength chaos. As a result, no one heard anything, nothing happened.

At one point, out of sheer despair, I decided to try and field the disharmony by surrendering to spiritual guidance. With scant hope of any result, I leaned back in my chair and began focusing on the Divine Light that formed each being in each seat around the table. There were several people present, so I was engrossed in this process for quite a while. No one noticed I had stepped back; no one cared—the fireworks were too compelling. So the nonsense went on outside while I did my spiritual work inside. Some time later, I noticed that I had become amazingly calm and steady, and shortly afterwards I turned my attention back to the meeting.

It was a different meeting. The fractiousness had evaporated into I don't know where, and the communication had slowly inched down to a viable pace. Most remarkable of all, simple listening had entered the picture. And since listening makes the whole difference between babble and resolution, all was now well.

I have no idea what the original argument was about (see how trivial these urgent issues are in the long run). But I do remember that an agreement was reached, and also that everyone left in a cheerful mood.

Now, let me be clear about this. This quiet process of blessing produced no divine revelations, no thunder from heaven—just cheerfulness. But those of you who have experienced quarrels during meetings will know that cheerfulness is miracle enough for anyone. And yes, it is a spiritual healing.

So the next time you find yourself in a group pickle and are ready to engage in some personal growth, I have two words for you:

Silent Blessing.

SO ALIKE, SO ALIKE

Oh yes, our packaging is
wildly different,
and the histories, too.
My journey began
under a blood-red moon,
yours under a rose-gold star.
But histories are just icing.

Histories may well curve
the shape of our footsteps,
or tint the tone of our song;
but never can they alter our Substance.
Nothing can touch Substance.
It is inviolable.

So here we amazingly are,
two discrete strings
on the same instrument;
both leaning gloriously into
One divine melody.

STEPPING BACK

Here in my hand is an ordinary marble. You've all seen one like it thousands of times. This particular one has a dazzling swirl of multi-colored veins frozen inside its smooth, glassy sphere. Rolling it lightly between my fingers, I am certain that nothing could possibly be sleeker to the touch.

Or so it seems.

And yet, when I place this same slight, round ball under a microscope, an entirely different world becomes visible. Suddenly, the once sleek surface offers up something new: jagged edges, mountainous crags, ditches, craters, veins. Magnified, the surface is now so uneven and disordered that I find myself blinking with surprise. And there is only one doorway out of this broken-up universe—to abandon the close-up view.

Sure enough, as soon as I take my eye away from the magnifying lens, the marble reappears, smooth as ever. Gleaming and orderly, a perfect sphere once again.

Of course there are times when we need to magnify something; the microscope and telescope are primary tools for observing the nature and makeup of matter. But in this instance I wasn't thinking about the useful functions of a microscope; I was noticing how easily magnification can distort our overview.

And the distortion occurs instantly, with the flick of an eye.

Just like in everyday life. You and I both know that we humans magnify stuff mentally all the time, and with not very happy results. We grab hold of life-bits and blow them up. We enlarge small incidents until our heads wobble and we have lost all perspective. It's called making a mountain out of a molehill. We magnify feelings into obsessions. We magnify a set of experiences or events into a rigid belief. We magnify insults. We magnify fears. We magnify differences.

Let's say we are magnifying a simple irritation. Here's how we proceed: gluing one eye tight to our mental microscope, we go over every inch of the occurrence; poring over its enlarged veins and landscape until it is embedded fever-like in our consciousness. Then, completely forgetting to remove our eye from the enlarging lens, we now move around in real space wearing the over-sized irritation around our neck like a pendant.

And when I say we have forgotten to look up from the microscope, I'm not kidding. In this mode, our mind is out to lunch; we forget we are looking close-up at the cells and veins of a small bit of life. We are lost. The irritation, once a small and hapless flicker in life's journey, is now so huge it has become the engine in our day. The car is driving us.

Of course, all it takes to bring things back to normal is to quick-step back from the magnifying agent and take a long, broad look at the whole landscape. Zap! The overblown bit is restored to its proper size again; we take a deep breath, and maybe a deep sigh, and remember flyspecks are flyspecks.

Relief floods over us now; it was all a bad dream. How could a flyspeck possibly drive us nuts?

I mean—unless we let it.

TRANSFORMATION

Once
I was high up in an airplane
which moved along the sky on such quiet feet
that I was able to remain in a state of prayer
the whole way with no effort.

Outside my window flew field after field
of impossibly puffed clouds, so innocent
they took my breath away.
I could feel their tenderness
without touching them —
round white vaporous flowers
lining the highway of the sky.

When the plane landed, I walked off
feeling inordinately blessed and calm.
Carrying my little bag into the airport,
I moved with a light step
and considered listening to Bach
when I got back home.
My ears and nose were perfectly in place —
all was exceedingly well.

The next thing I knew,
I was in a hurricane of movement
— voices, rushings, announcements,
frenzies of all descriptions.
My link with the sacred trembled and fell away.
I was back in this world.

There is no question that this world pulls
at us with hypnotic intensity; coaxes us into
its clamors with a thousand and one invitations.
And there is no question that we will surrender
here and there and then and now to its pull.
It happens a thousand times a day;
it will happen a thousand times tomorrow.

So how do we do it, those of us who are
committed to a deeper, more numinous calling;
who have responded to an inner invitation
to explore the sacred?
How do we travel in our mundane world,
given over to noise and excitement
and frenzy and happenstance—
and still witness the Divine? Here's what I do.
I use prayer and prayer and prayer
to keep the door open.
Aside from that, we can do nothing.
What else is there to do?
I think the only reason
we ever see the Divine at all
is because the Divine chooses to let us see It.
Our part is to remember to honor the Silence
—that opens the door.

Once we have thus expressed our will
to see the sacred, the sacred shows its face.
Not when we say, show yourself!
but more often when we have stopped
saying anything, and simply handed ourselves

over for filling up.
Then is when we are ready.

And there it is,
a secret, sacred heaven,
hidden behind the broiling, roiling universe.
Never will we see it with human eyes;
all we can do is prepare the way with silence.
And wait.

And catch our breath when it appears.

Waking Up

Of course, most of us
wake up slowly, slowly,
one eye growing wider and clearer,
while the other stays firmly fixed
on the dream we were just enjoying.
We thought that dream was real,
and we long for its coziness,
its mysterious liquid motion.

But one eye is partly open.
Too late to sink back fully into the dream.
Not knowing quite what to do,
we burrow deeper into our blankets,
borrowing their warmth,
and sigh over the brightness
of the sun.
Oh yes, we want the sun,
all of us want the sun.
But not yet, not yet.
Not at the expense
of comfort.

It's not that we are foolish.
It's just that we don't trust the New
and we don't know for sure
that even sweet dreams carry less joy
than Oneness.
So we pause.

Still, the Awakening will happen.
God does not leave us loitering
in dark alleys forever.
He sees our barely opening eye,
our faint wondering,
our hunger for wholeness,
and in one unsuspecting moment,
with a sudden thrust of heart,
He pulls us into His Arms.

WATER LESSONS

I'm walking on the beach,
curling sand under my toes
just for the heat of it,
and listening to the water.
I love listening to water.
It is prehistoric music
sung by a force that is at home
with its own liquidity;
a celebration of wetness.

I love water because it moves
with gentleness, fluidity and power
all at the same time.
And it has something else—
a stark certainty of purpose.
Knowing raised to an art.
That's how water lives.

But we ... we do it differently.
We humans are too clever to hear
our inner biddings full tilt.
We have histories, habits, patterns
blocking our view.
With all earnestness, we try
to hear the whispers of God
through our own interior barriers,
which so often muddle the message.

Water doesn't question or translate.
Water is simply sure.

Just watch the sea with me—
it rises, reaches, surges forward,
dances in joy for a long moment
and then recedes with slow elegance,
all in response to the call of the moon.

And it's all done without trappings;
no instructions are needed.
The connection is relentlessly clear;
each motion perfect.
The moon and the sea are one;
and that's all there is to it.

I am one with God,
but being less certain than water,
more distracted, more programmed
more interruptive in my attention,
I hear only sometimes.

I watch this dancing water
teach me clarity,
and here's how my prayer goes:
I want to know God from my gut
in every now,
the way a single sleek wave
moment after moment
leaps up without hesitation
to taste the distant moon.

WHY WE'RE HERE

Imagine
a brilliantly colored world atlas
spread out, vast as a tablecloth,
across your dining room table.

You stand before it, peering at its
endless nooks and crannies,
its giant pools of blue water, looking over
the exotic and unfathomable names of cities
and countries beyond your awareness.
You take in the whole of this mammoth map,
parts of which are familiar as dust,
parts of which are completely alien.

And pretend you've been given an assignment
to bless and forgive every piece of this huge map;
every name, every river, every mountain,
every desert,
every village, every spa, every bridge, every coast,
every battleground, every street sign.

Now you can stop pretending.
Because in truth that's exactly the way it is.
You and I have been given such an assignment—
to forgive everything, everyone, everywhere.
That is our human potential.

You ask: but with a world that stretches
so many miles out of sight, with such an

immense list of characters and events,
how on earth do we accomplish such a
herculean task?

Piece by piece by piece.

Actually, it's simpler than it seems.
Simpler, but not easier.
This world is much like a hologram,
which means that to entirely forgive
and bless the small piece of map
on which we stand and live
is to forgive the whole.

So we start right where we are.
Day by day, we are here to learn to see past
what our eyes and ears report;
to see through surface to essence.

We are learning to forgive it all.
The ripe lush strawberry that made us itch.
The pothole that tore a hole in our tire.
The grocery clerk with an attitude.
The relatives we try to avoid.
The co-worker who appears to hate us.
The newspaper report of a gang shooting.
The water bill that is inordinately high.
The washing machine that shrank
our sweater into a doll's dress.
The driver that splashed mud on our new jacket.
The sun that refused to come out
when we needed it.

The endlessly long line at our favorite restaurant.
The head that blocked our view at a concert.
The checkbook that doesn't add up.
The irate letter from a landlord.

Everything.

These are our daily assignments;
the extraordinary opportunities we are given
to see past the skin of all moments
and catch the shining innocence that waits beyond
and beneath the obvious.

Is it easy work? No.
Does it take a long time to complete? Yes.
But of course we are given a lifetime
in which to do it.

And when we have moved through our
private map, piece by piece by piece, and
with the help of the Divine Love at our center
have come to release each face, each instance,
each folly—what happens then?

Freedom.

ZEN BREAKFAST

In front of me is a cup of new hot coffee and a fresh bagel. The bagel holds a delicate strip of pink lox resting lightly on a bed of cream cheese.

I'm hungry, so the taste is especially good — more than good. At this moment, it seems like the perfect food. Appetite has sharpened my awareness, and each bite is a delicious surprise, one after the other. The miracle of these disparate elements coming together in one Lucullan blend floors me.

I think, how many other small treasures would increase in depth and beauty if I took the time to look at them fully, the way I am now looking at this breakfast? How many times am I not seeing because I am looking with unopened eyes?

It is obvious to me that I do this — look without seeing. I know it because I can tell the difference when I do otherwise. Possibly it is sheer laziness that keeps me from doing it all the time; I have some chores to do, I want to sleep through them, so rather than staying intent and conscious of the moments in front of me, I slip into automatic pilot. I nap.

When I do this, my internal machinery steers the ship; it knows its job. Three hours later the chores are done, but without the participation of my self. It seems like a good enough transaction; things got done, didn't they? And yet ...

There is another reason I sometimes nap: my instinctive wish to avoid the things I don't like. Listening to a conversation that seems trivial, for instance, may cause me to move my mind elsewhere and let my head nod at appropriate intervals. Doing this, I think I am saving myself from boredom.

The truth is, going unconscious saves nothing; whenever I sleep, I am the loser. Things get done, yes, but any joys inherent in the process slip by without my noticing. And here is the worst news: when my self is not there, there is no force present to alter or amend the event itself.

For example, I used to hate going to the dentist. I would enter the office with a grimace, endure the whole appointment with narrowed eyes and tightened jaw, and walk out like a human fist on legs.

But one day, as I sat in the waiting room deep in aversion to the moments ahead, I did something different. I stopped myself from going to sleep in self-defense. As best I could, I relaxed every muscle in my body. I closed my eyes, took some authentic breaths, and began to appreciate the chair I was sitting on. With my breath in full operation, my focus was intense, and I could actually feel the kindness of the cushion I rested on and the arms that supported my elbows. Think of the generosity of that support! My feet had a comfortable floor holding them up; there was faint music playing on the intercom. It was clear to me that the music had only one purpose—to soothe me. I began to sink into what felt like a river of safety.

By the time they called me into the small room where sharp instruments and cold jets of water awaited me, I was no longer tense with fear. Believe it or not, I was able to see those strange silver tools as friends and the jets of water as a sidebar blessing. The dentist seemed utterly harmless; a helpful mechanic putting things in order quickly and quietly. I felt an enormous fondness for his skill and silence.

Perhaps it will not surprise you when I tell you that this appointment flew by in minutes and I felt no pain or distress whatever throughout the treatment.

And that's what can happen when the Self stays present. When I am looking very, very closely at a given moment—free of aversion, free of fear, free of memories, free of judgment, free of barriers—the moment suddenly steps out of its box and becomes a gift.

Funny, isn't it, how often large lessons come from small events.

Stay awake.

ON DISCERNING THE RIPE PLUM

One of the most revered of the ancient Zen Buddhist teachers was a man named Hui-neng. It is said that during his life he reached very, very far into God and that realization first came to him when he was still a child.

As a very young boy, Hui-neng was drawn to serve in the peaceful mountain monastery of the Yellow Plum, a Zen Buddhist Order in China. Since he was illiterate and considered far too young and ignorant to begin serious studies, he was put to work pounding rice in the kitchen.

Then, barely a year after Hui-neng began his work in the kitchen, the old patriarch of the Yellow Plum Order announced that the time had come for him to choose a successor. He invited all his young monks to submit poems for a competition. The object was to see which monk had realized the highest expression of Truth.

Among the contenders, there was a monk by the name of Shen-shiu who was considered by far the most learned student present. Everyone agreed his poem would probably win. Shen-shiu wrote:

> This body is the Bodhi-tree,
> The mind, a mirror bright.
> Take care to wipe them always clean,
> Less dust on them alight.

The night before the winner was to be announced, a friendly young monk read the prize verse to the illiterate kitchen boy, Hui-neng. After he had heard it, Hui-neng asked his friend to write down a verse to place beside the one written by Shen-shiu. This was the verse spoken by Hui-neng:

> There never was a Bodhi-tree,
> Nor any mirror bright.
> Since nothing
> At the root exists,
> On what should dust alight?

And that is the story of how the illiterate Hui-neng came to be selected by the old Zen patriarch as his successor.

In Which We Remember the Script Has a Happy Ending

Remember what happens when you use an alarm to wake yourself up? The buzzer sounds (per your instructions), so you shut it off. Then you slip back into a snooze, dream some ten-second dreams, and bolt back awake. And then repeat the process a second time, or a third. Maybe even a sixth. Then—Pow! You jump up, you're awake, you're alive; you go on about your day.

That's how it is, waking up from our dreams at night. And waking up from our dream of separation happens much the same way.

We receive, at some point, a realization of our spiritual identity. It seems to flood through us like a laser beam—something within us has come awake. So we step, pulled by some internal magnet, onto the Path.

Yet soon after, we find we have slipped back into our old dream of a separate self, where fear seems real, and folks seem this or that, and God is some distant, barely visible star on our horizon. The world looms large.

Suddenly we remember, "I dozed off again!" And taking a deep breath, we return to Self.

So we proceed, most of us, in and out of sleep: nodding off, becoming Conscious! Nodding off, becoming Conscious! Nodding off, becoming Conscious!

And yes, this seesaw movement can feel frustrating, particularly because while a morning snooze lasts no longer than ten or twenty minutes, our spiritual nodding off and waking up can seem to go on for years.

But here's the good news: no matter how long we seem to teeter between this world and heaven; no matter how often we slip back into the old, separated way of seeing things, our drowsy state is finite. It does not go on forever. Though the world mind is stunningly seductive and pulls at all of us all the time, its pull doesn't last. It can't.

It wasn't made by God. But here's what was made by God: our Real Self, created inconquerable, infinite, whole and free. And that is Who shines forth after our false facade has faded from our sight.

Of course, knowing the outcome doesn't mean we can neglect our practice. Au contraire! Practice is our door to freedom. But it does mean don't be discouraged. When you slip back into darkness for a brief (or not-so-brief) moment, take heart. As our old friend Emerson once said, "God's dice are always loaded."

ॐ ॐ

"Time is an illusion perpetrated by the manufacturers of space."　　　—Graffiti

How Can You Ever Lose
ORANGE?

Oh, orange! That vibrant dawn and citrus hue; that shotgun marriage of red and yellow! Orange is bright, orange is stark, orange is definite. But think: does not orange have one quality worth noting above all others? It is simply always here. Present or not present to my eye, orange is alive; orange is being orange, in every moment you can name and every moment you can't name. Here it stands, resting in the one Mind. Ready to dance whenever we call it forth. Oh, yes! The universe hums with orangeability.

Nevertheless, nevertheless. I can seem to have a day without orange. So can you. No question— orange can seem to escape us. Deprived of orange groves, for example, I can appear to lose the form that orange imbues. But that is all I can lose. Orange itself is ever now; way more perpetual than taxes. And orange cannot be misplaced, destroyed, injured, or marred in anyway. It certainly can't be lost.

And neither can You.

Nor can you lose Life.

Nor can you lose Nourishment.

Nor can you lose Love.

Nor can you lose Joy.

Nor can you lose Home.

Or rainbows.

Why? Because, like you, they are all spiritual. God, the Indescribable One, is nonmaterial, and all that issues from His eternal essence is like Himself: inviolate, invisible, infinite. Spirit walks on weightless feet, and the laws of Spirit apply everywhere, to everything.

Bach heard symphonies even when his human ears had deserted him. Why? Because true hearing is a function of Spirit, not eardrums.

So never fear the loss of form. Form is simply an after-effect, a shadow self, from whose presence we can infer the Real Thing. As a damp shoreline infers the sea; as a fingerprint infers a hand; as a bread crust infers a meal; as a rose infers beauty. But what we want is to experience the Is of a thing. And to do that, we get still and go where? Inside.

Forms come. Forms go. The Real Thing can— and does—cast a thousand imprints, and a thousand more. So long as you need them, imprints will appear and disappear. But that which the imprint points to—the Essence—is forever present, forever being Itself.

༖ ༖

"There wouldn't be such a thing as counterfeit gold if there were no real gold somewhere."

—Sufi proverb

My Introduction to the God Glasses

I'll never forget the first time I visited Angel Island, that other-dimensional place where angels hang out, keeping an eye on things, on call to lend a hand. My first surprise? How ordinary they looked. There they were, walking around in sundry shapes and sizes, just like us. Of course, their clothing was kind of look-alike; trendless, you might say, but that's because they don't bother about it much.

Anyway, I was wandering around the place, wearing my visitor's badge, taking it all in — angels goofing off, angels consulting on problem cases, angels meditating, angels laughing, angels growing flowers. It could have been earth, except for this odd hum of well-being that permeated the air. Whenever you breathed in, a kind of champagne rush bathed you all over. It left a lightness in your toes.

I came to this one official-looking place (Help Headquarters they call it) and marched on in. There was a lobby, hallways, and lots of conference rooms. I popped into one of them and found two senior-looking angels intently watching a movie screen.

"Hey, looks like a close-up of Planet Earth," I said. "It is," they replied. The film was showing a big time businessman, mega-rich by the looks of his suit, ordering lunch at his power desk. The desk was piled to the ceiling with papers. Phones were ringing, underlings were rushing in and out carrying memos. The guy was barking orders, pulling rank—all the things people of power get to do and other people don't. The underlings all had resentment lines etched in their foreheads. I sighed; it was such a familiar scene. I've been in offices like that. Hasn't everyone?

Next up onscreen, in comes this battered old delivery guy from the delicatessen, carrying a neat white paper bag. Lunch for the Big Guy. Big Guy takes the lunch, throws a ten at the oldster and waves him away, with a "You're nobody" glance. The old guy gives him some change, beams him a shockingly big smile, and exits.

"The powerful and the weak. I've seen scenes like that a hundred times," I said.

"Yeah, but you haven't seen it with the God-glasses," they told me, and passed along a pair of those glasses you get in 3-D movies. "Good grief!" I think, "What's this gimmick?" I put them on.

I look up at the screen, and now it's completely 360 degrees different. Same film, same scene, but now suddenly there's this amazing plot switch.

Where the Big Guy used to be sitting at his mammoth, high-octane desk, there is just a tiny, frail, barely-flickering little light. And there's a sound coming from this baby-sized flicker, a sad little "Help-me, Help-me" singsong. And where the old delivery guy used to be is this huge dazzling column of light, spreading like a sunburst all over the little "Help-me" flicker at the desk. After the column shines for a few moments, the flicker gets a little stronger, burns a little brighter. As soon as the flicker looks firm, the blazing column of light leaves.

"Oh," I said, "right. The God-glasses—how it looks to God."

On Angel Island, wonders never cease.

DO LESS, BE MORE

Have you ever watched a fan running at incredibly high speed? It builds slowly, moving with greater and greater intensity, until it is whirling so furiously and so fast that the blades simply disappear into a single blur.

So, do the blades really evaporate when the blur has swallowed them up? Of course not. But they do seem absent.

And isn't that precisely what happens to us when our human mind starts running at dizzying speed? It, too, forms a blur, hiding our real Self. If, that is, we're caught up in it.

Some have reached the point where their peace is untroubled, no matter what. For others, this is the season when getting caught up in world-stuff is perilously easy. Nothing sets off the blades of human thought quicker than a holiday, tempting us into human expectations, human complaints, human motion: parties, shopping, family reunions, feasts, travel, angst. Come December, the race for external joys begins in earnest, and temptation after temptation flies into our path. More human buttons get pushed at Christmas, say the experts, than any other time of the year. Small wonder so many end up exhausted; external pursuits always leave us feeling somehow empty, as though we were missing something. And if we are running fast, without pausing to go within for divine fuel, then indeed we *are* missing something—our Self.

Christmas is a simple metaphor for the birth of the Christ within us. Yet that birth can only happen in an arena uncluttered by human thought and human concerns. Time and again, it occurs in the simplest, sparest room in our Consciousness—Silence.

So as holiday events flutter their many-colored ribbons before us and beckon us to run along beside them, let's give ourselves an important gift: space for I Am. Let's stop and pause—often—to drink from the infinite well of Christ. For only His presence, alive in our hearts, can keep us free from the hypnotic, frantic blades of this world.

Use silence as a cleanser; wash yourself with it every day, every night, every hour, so that there is always a clear space through which the Christ may radiate. At that point, there will be no need for you to seek joy. No need at all—for you will *be* joy.

൏ ൙

"The fabled musk deer searches the world over for the source of the scent which comes from itself."

—Ramakrishna

IS ANYONE HERE?

A wise and revered teacher lay dying on his bed, and a few chosen disciples had been invited in to meditate with him during his last hours on earth.

After a brief time they were all asked to leave except one, a brilliant and devoted student named Asha. Thus, when everyone else had bowed and filed out, Asha went over and knelt beside the Master, thrilled and proud at being chosen to share a few private moments with the Awakened One. To be given such an honor! Asha was flushed with delight.

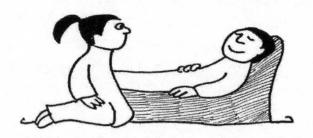

He knelt quietly in prayer beside the Master's bed. A half hour passed by in complete silence, then an hour more. Asha began to wonder if his teacher had fallen asleep. But no, at last the old

Master said quietly from his bed, "Is anyone here?"

And Asha quickly replied. "Yes, Master, it is I, Asha, right here beside you."

The Master said nothing. Another hour of deep silence went by, then another, then another, then another. After this long time in silence, the old Master finally asked again: "Is anyone here?"

Once again Asha whispered, "Yes, Master, it is I, Asha."

The Master said, "Oh, you're still here, Asha? Well, let me know when you're not here anymore, so that there's plenty of room for the One."

—Ancient Buddhist tale

WHEN THINGS GO
BUMP IN THE NIGHT

One of the greatest mystical jokes of all time is the one delivered by Woody Allen at the end of his film *Annie Hall*. Remember it? It went like this:

A guy goes to his doctor and says, "My brother really needs some help. He thinks he's a chicken." And the doctor says, "Well, why on earth don't you bring him in for some treatment?" And the guy says, "Because we need the eggs."

That's it. That's it exactly. That's why we can still get caught sometimes. Why we still get frightened at things that go bump in the night. It's because, even knowing that the chicken is an illusion, there's a part of us that thinks maybe (anything's possible, right?) we can use it.

So there we are, minding our own business, and a blip of distressing news crosses our life screen. Familiar with the letter of truth, we're quick to see it's the false self reporting the blip. "This is just more of the 'me' mirage," we tell ourself. And yet!—much as we'd like to see it dissolve into nothingness, there's a teeny-tiny part of us still holding onto the false self that's doing the mischief.

So it's possible to find ourselves, at times, in the curious position of praying on the one hand to have our dark perceptions lifted and, on the other hand, still keeping a fingertip wound around the false self. Why? Because we think we need the eggs.

Yes, I know it's insane. But there it is. Even while we're asking the I Am to reveal Itself, here comes that luckless human mind, still whispering in our ear that the false self can amount to something. Do something. Be something. Earn something. Learn something.

And it can't.

Which is why we've been given the die daily advice so often. That die daily advice is no joke, and it's not a halfway measure. We're either Spirit, or we're dreaming we're a body. We can't be both. We're either born of God, or dreaming we're born of man. We can't be both.

So the next time you're tempted to hold on to the false self because you think you need the eggs, remember, you don't. Forget the chicken. Go for the bliss.

Die daily.

༄ ༅

"Put not your trust in princes, nor in the son of man, in whom there is no help."

—Psalms 146:3

PURIFICATION

Once there was a disciple of a renowned Greek philosopher who was handed an odd assignment. He was commanded by his master to give money to everyone who insulted him, for a period of three years. Wanting very much to awaken, this student did exactly as he was told. When this rather lengthy trial was over, the Master summoned the young man to his quarters and said to him, "Now you can go to Athens, for you are ready to learn wisdom."

Elated, the disciple set off for Athens. Just before he entered the great city, he saw a certain wise man sitting at the gate insulting everybody who came and went. Naturally, the moment this fellow saw the disciple, he insulted him, too.

"Hey!" he cried out to the student, "how did you get to be so ugly and stupid? I have never before seen anyone as ridiculous looking as you."

But instead of taking offense, the disciple just burst out laughing.

"Why do you laugh when I insult you?" asked the wise man.

"Because," said the disciple, "for three whole years I have been paying for this kind of thing and now you give it to me for nothing!"

"Enter the city," said the wise man, "it is all yours."

—Desert Fathers

THE SAD ROOM

This wonderful old story has been stored in my memory for countless years, but I honestly don't remember which angel first told it to me.

It seems that a certain fellow named Josh (for reasons known only to the mysterious workings of the Celestial Order) was granted in mid-life a brief, sudden visit to heaven, and, even more amazing, an actual live audience with God.

Upon Josh's arrival, God appeared as promised and offered to give him a tour of the Upper Regions. He then took Josh to a series of delightful and delicious places: music rooms, halls of painting, breathtaking cloud retreats, quiet, evergreen gardens of meditation, banquet halls, and even an angel gym. Each was far more splendid than Josh had ever expected, and he was duly awed.

Naturally, this being a brief visit, he could in no way see everything; an infinite number of places takes a very long while to visit. So after a brief sample of heavenliness, the visitor was gently escorted back toward the entrance to Earth. Along the way, they passed a certain tall, hand-carved doorway which was so spectacular a sight that Josh stopped before it, spellbound.

"What's in there?" he asked, riveted. And God said, "Oh, please, don't ask me about that room. I hate to go in there. It's the Sad Room."

But Josh was undaunted. "Oh, Sir," he replied, "I've never seen such a beautiful doorway in my life. Won't you please let me look inside?"

At first God just shook His head. But after considerable pleading from Josh, He finally relented. "All right, all right. I'll take you inside."

Raising a large, intricate key from the folds of His gown, He opened the majestic door and ushered His guest within. Once inside, Josh's jaw dropped, for the vast room before him was a veritable storehouse of priceless treasures. It was crammed wall to wall with table after table filled with stunning wares: superb artwork, pure gold table settings, rare jewelry, gem-laden sculptures, pure crystal—dazzling objets d'art that took the breath away. When, after a moment, he could finally speak again, Josh cried out, "But all this is unbelievably beautiful! Why do you call it the Sad Room?"

And sighing deeply, God said, "It's called the Sad Room, because this is where I store the treasures I have tried to give to my children, but they were too fearful to accept."

HOW TO KILL TRUTH

One day Mara, who is the ancient Buddhist god of ignorance and evil, was traveling through the villages of India with his attendants. Along the way, he noticed a man doing a walking meditation. The man's face was lit up in wonder. Apparently, the man had just discovered something on the ground in front of him.

Mara's attendants, noticing the glow emanating from the man, asked Mara what it was the man had discovered. Mara replied, "He has discovered a piece of truth."

"But Evil One!" exclaimed one of his entourage, "doesn't this bother you when someone finds a piece of the truth?"

"No," said Mara. "I am not troubled in the least."

"But why not?" insisted his attendants.

"Because," replied Mara, chuckling, "right after they discover some truth, they usually make a belief out of it."

— Ancient Buddhist tale

RELATIONSHIPS 101

Recently I had the good fortune to witness a Buddhist wedding ceremony; it was stunningly stark and beautiful. Among the vows made were these three:

"I vow to refrain from all actions that create attachment. I vow to make every effort to live awake and in the truth. I vow to live to benefit all beings."

Afterwards, I asked the Zen priest about the purpose of the attachment vow, since marriage is clearly an attachment. And he said, "That vow is made to remind the couple that their marriage is, above all else, a teaching tool. It is through their closeness that they can learn to put aside the small self, which is finite, and move into their True Self, which is boundless."

And we all know this is so. Relationships, particularly close ones, give us an immense opportunity to see the Unseeable, provided, of course, we are paying attention. Which means remembering Who stands before us.

Not an easy thing to do when we are looking through the lens of littleness. In fact, it's impossible to see Who is there through the limited human lens, for its view is perpetually dark.

But! We can put aside that lens and look through Spirit. Simply put, the gift another being gives us (if we can accept it) is the opportunity to heal our own darkness.

So here's what to do with this week, this month, this lifetime: pick someone, anyone, and practice seeing the Divine in that one. Practice without ceasing.

Remember, this is not about seeing a "good" human being. This is about seeing beyond all humanness, all personalness, all history, and keeping the eye of your heart focused on the Holy Self who lies hidden behind the human mask.

Then begin your work to see the Perfect One in this being, no matter what. Be faithful to your task; it is a daily exercise. And the miracle is—this being, this teacher, will begin to unfold before you in a way that is so huge, so deep, and so beyond words that you will never again see him or her in a small way.

And more than that—as you persist, as you continue, as you hold to your vision day after day after day, you will come to an immense realization that the radiance you are seeing is your Self.

BEYOND RULES

Once upon a morning many years ago, a renowned Taoist master was sitting naked in his mountain cabin, meditating. A small group of Confucianists hiked up the mountain to visit him, intending to lecture him on the rules of proper conduct in spiritual practice. Entering the door of his hut, they stopped short, for seeing the sage sitting naked before them shocked them one and all. When they caught their breath, they asked him, "What are you doing, sitting in your hut without any pants on?"

And the sage replied, "The entire universe is my hut. This little hut is my pants. What are you fellows doing inside my pants?"

Where Could I Go?

In honor of Luella

Some years ago, after a lifetime of deep service, an important and much beloved spiritual teacher took ill. Over a period of weeks it became clear he was ready to leave his body and return to the One. Moments like these are not easy ones, and many of his students had gathered near his bedside during this time, wanting to remain close in the last days. Some students remained calm and in peace, while others were openly in tears over the prospect of losing their priceless Friend and Guide. One such student bent close to the Teacher's ear and whispered passionately:

"Oh, Babaji, Babaji, please don't leave us!"

The teacher chuckled and then slowly turned his face and looked straight into the eyes of the weeping student, saying:

"Don't be silly! Where could I go?"

RETREAT FOR ONE

We've all been lucky enough to attend class retreats, so I don't need to tell you about the illimitable glow that follows after and suffuses our daily life.

Yet, for this reason or that, sometimes there is a long, long space between the classes we can attend. And what do we do then, if the world seems to be looming large?

We can do a retreat on our own, a private meeting with I Am. It is an experience that may surprise you with its intensity.

The requirements are simple. All you need is one weekend, or even one day, and a commitment to silence. Truth is within you always, waiting for your listening ear.

Location? You can do it anywhere—at home, in the country, in the desert, in the mountains, in your backyard. God never cares what phone booth you call from.

Remember—bring no rulers, no charts to test for results, for there is no sure way to measure what happens in the Silence. Over time, yes, you may get a sense of discovered Truth, for without question, the Spirit does impact our living.

But if we are looking for results, we are by definition assuming our material life and its problems are solid and real. They are not.

And it is precisely to heal our minds of this painful misperception that we are appealing to Silence in the first place.

So forget the world. Forget it. Let it go. Release it out of your two hands as you would free a wild bird.

On a personal retreat there is but one assignment: to experience His Presence. To sink into It, revel in It, so that It can open us to the experience of Love and then extend through us to bless all who are free to receive It.

Sometimes it strikes me that our human selves are much like the little extraterrestrial in Steven Spielberg's gentle film, caught for no reason in a strange and fear-ridden planet which is unable to see its Soul.

Isn't it like that? On the human level, aren't we all ET, longing for another place, an ancient sense of belonging?

ET, call Home.

℘ ℀

"Who then tells a finer tale than any of us? Silence does."

—Isak Dinesen

THE TEACHER

During the years when the great mystic Gurdjieff ran his spiritual community in Europe, hundreds and hundreds of students came to study with him. The work of awakening was hard and rigorous, and not surprisingly, a deep kinship soon developed among the students who lived there.

Or at least, among almost all of them.

For there was a notable exception. On one occasion, there arrived a student who was distinctly different from the rest. He was a surly old man with a hideously unpleasant manner. He was so obnoxious, in fact, that in no time at all he had repelled the entire community. His fellow students found him rude, ill-tempered, uncooperative and unabashedly self-centered. One by one, serious students went to Gurdjieff and complained about the old man. "We're here doing dedicated work," they would say, "and this idiot is making all of us unhappy. You've got to expel him!"

But Gurdjieff simply chuckled and waved the complainers away.

However, so intensely did the students detest the old man that one by one they began to ostracize him. Heads turned away when he entered the room. No one would greet him. Day after day he was wrapped in a strange, communal silence. After several months of this treatment, the surly old man caved in and left the community.

Gone! Vanished! Absent forever! When word came that the ogre was gone, the students were overjoyed.

However, when Gurdjieff heard what had happened, he immediately packed up his bags and followed him. Finally, he tracked the man down, knocked on his door and asked to speak to him.

"Why did you leave, old fellow?" he asked.

"You know they all hate me!" snapped the old man. "I couldn't take it anymore."

"Well," said Gurdjieff, "Tell you what. If you'll come back and live with us again, I'll make amends for all you've suffered. In fact, I'll pay you a handsome salary for as long as you agree to stay."

Mollified by this generous offer, and keenly aware that the other students paid large fees to stay in the community, the old man immediately chose to return with Gurdjieff.

Oh, day of horror! When the students saw that their nemesis had once again returned to the community, they were furious. Whole groups of them rushed into Gurdjieff's room to protest. "And we hear you're actually paying him money to stay!" they cried, "Yet the rest of us, who are far more advanced, have to pay substantial monies to be here!" Outrage flooded the room.

In reply, Gurdjieff merely threw back his head and laughed.

"Of course I pay him!" he roared. "Have you forgotten you're here to learn non-judgment? Show a little respect, you numbskulls—this old man is one of the most perfect teachers you'll ever find!"

THE GIFT

It arrived every day, rain or shine, in oddly shaped boxes. The boxes were oddly shaped because the gift itself was never exactly the same. One day it would be loose and light as a cloud, yet on another day it would be as fierce as flames, or flow like a river on the next; on still another day it would whistle and flutter, or perhaps glisten like the inside of a shell.

In the beginning, he opened up each package eagerly, tearing away the wrappings with great wonder, laughing at the surprise of it, the lilt of it, at how it was both light and solid, quick and slow at the same time.

That was in the beginning. After a while, though, something happened. He found his interest beginning to dull ever so subtly. He would open the gift later in the day, towards afternoon, perhaps. Then he might leave it untouched until after dinner. Later on, he found himself delaying the opening until right before he went to sleep. Eventually the day came when he had a pile of unopened gifts, stacked one upon the other, leaning against his closet wall.

"Well, I'm tired of opening these boxes," he would explain to himself. "Yes, they'll all be fine, all of them. But I have serious work to do. How can I be bothered with opening gifts?"

And so, with his thoughts running along this unfortunate line, one morning he did the unthinkable. When the knock came upon his door, telling him the gift had arrived, he went to the door and waved the messenger away. "Take it back," he said. "I don't want it. I already have a thousand just like it."

Without a word, the messenger plucked up the gift and disappeared from view.

Days went by. The knock never came again; no more gifts came to the door. Yet as the weeks passed, he noticed an unhappy ache growing in the pit of his stomach. I miss the gifts, he thought; and he did—he missed the fresh shock of them, the warmth of their song. And the ache didn't go away; bit by bit it deepened into longing. At last, unable to bear his feelings of loss, he went to see an old wise man. He told him the story of his mysterious gifts and how they stopped coming.

"Mmmm," said the wise man, after listening to the tale. "Of course they stopped coming! A gift of that caliber is one you must never refuse, because it cannot come without your welcome."

"But I had so much on hand!" he said, trying to offer an explanation. "And so much else to do."

The old man laughed. "Without the gift, your doing is meaningless," he said. "And how can you possibly have too much? With a gift as precious as this one, you must give it away to keep it alive, and then embrace the next gift with open arms."

"I didn't know who would want it," he said. "I never knew what it was in the first place."

"And do you know what it is now?" asked the old man.

"Well, no," he said. "All I remember is it was such an odd gift—always the same, yet never alike; always new, yet somehow familiar. What was it, exactly?"

"The part of you which is always present but rarely seen," said the wise man. "And Its name is Love."

ჽ ᶜᴖ

"The experience of love arises when we surrender our separateness into the universal. It is a feeling of unity. You don't love another; you *are* another. There is no fear because there is no separation."

—Stephen Levine

TAKING TIME FOR THE TIMELESS

The days tick by, one, two, three, four, and after a bit we find a full year of them have flown behind us, over and out. And now here comes a new batch ... all neat and clean, stacked in the exact same order as before. Ready to chase down our human assembly line and insert a fresh new year. But first, let's celebrate over having gotten past last year's crop of days so tidily! And with such good humor.

Or maybe not. Here's a better idea: maybe we should skip all those gala parties we hold in honor of time. Possibly what we truly need is to pause and celebrate Something far more miraculous than a year full of dead days—like Timelessness.

Think about it. No-Time, like its cousin No-Thing, has been around a lot, lot longer than Time and Thing, and will be here way, way after Thing and Time have poofed themselves into thin air.

So, really, how about a celebration of *that*?

Particularly when we remember what's actually what in Reality. To Timelessness, things and time zones are just harmless dots of dandelion fluff floating around for a few blinks of an eye. Musing on that does provide a certain perspective on what's valuable and what's, well ... mere dandelion fluff.

How about it? Are you up for a moment wider than sky, deeper than time? Good—let's join together for a totally silent celebration of What Is. There's absolutely nothing holding us back. We can honor Timelessness together. You in your time zone, me in mine—with only imaginary walls between us—we can reach into Now and touch in one unclockable heartbeat.

So let's do it. Let's do it this second. Afterwards, perhaps you'll feel an inner sigh. Perhaps I'll feel an inner smile. It doesn't matter, we've both gotten our sign that we've been There. Touched base with the Infinite, bathed in No-Thingness, been present with the Timeless, the All.

Now, that's something worth rejoicing over.

"It is not hard to live through a day, if you can live through a moment. What creates despair is the imagination, which pretends there is a future, and insists on predicting millions of moments, thousands of days, and so drains you that you cannot live the moment at hand."

—Andre Dubus

The Prisoner

He came faithfully every week, a little man in nondescript clothing carrying some books and a bulging sack across his shoulder. He stopped at the gatehouse, signed his name to a slip of paper, and then waited still as night until the guard let him enter the main prison building. Once there, he spoke to another guard and finally was escorted down a dark, dank hallway to a cell.

Inside the cell sat the one he came to visit. Tall and thin, the man sat expressionless on his bunk. Narrow shoulders jutted forward as if warding off a blow. His dark eyes gleamed like small sapphires frozen in a piece of rock.

The old man entered the cell, nodded to the prisoner and sat down on the bunk beside him. Opening his sack, he carefully removed two pieces of fruit, a substantial sandwich, and a slice of cake. After handing these treasures to the prisoner, he then opened one of his worn books and began reading aloud. It was not a complicated reading, simply a page of prayers. He read the words in a voice so knowing that the sheer power of it appeared to hold the prisoner captive. Not once while the old man was reading did his listener reach for the tempting food that lay beside him.

An hour or so passed in this way, and at the end of that time the old man gathered his books together and got up to leave. As he walked out the cell door, he turned and waved to the man he left behind. Wasn't it true that the prisoner's eyes were a little lighter now? In fact, didn't his whole face seem freer somehow, despite the bars surrounding him? Or do we simply imagine it?

As the old man passed out through the front gate, one of the guards called him over.

"Why do you come here every week, old man?" he asked. "This prisoner will probably be here for a long, long time—he may never get out. Why on earth do you take all this trouble for a nobody?"

"Oh, but he isn't a nobody!" replied the old man. "Far from it! He's the most precious being I know—my own Self."

How to Fool a Giant

Probably all of you have heard the story of how elephants are trained for the circus. Still, it's worth telling again, I think, since it reveals to us so much about the shattering consequences of a deeply held belief.

How do they get an elephant to stand still in one place? Here's how: skilled trainers take the young elephant and wrap a chain around one of his baby legs, then lock the chain to a huge tree. For countless days, the tiny elephant tugs and tugs and tugs to free itself, but no matter how hard he pulls, he finds breaking loose utterly impossible. The chain is relentless, the tree too massive to yield. After days and weeks of failed attempts to break loose, the baby elephant at last settles down and accepts its fate.

Later, the trainers remove the heavy chain and use only a strong cord around the elephant's leg, which they attach to a much smaller tree. Does the elephant notice? No, he no longer makes any move to free himself, because he remembers profoundly the times when all his attempts were useless.

Time passes; the elephant matures.

And when he is fully grown, this same elephant can be tied up with nothing stronger than a slight piece of twine affixed to a young stripling no larger than the size of a broom handle. By now, of course, the elephant is an animal of awesome strength; the truth is, he could free himself instantly with one small kick of his foot. Yet, look at the amazing psychological grip which holds him still!

The ancient memory of all his fruitless attempts to break away have imprinted themselves deeply on his will and made him blind to his own power. Now he stays obediently in place, held captive by a thread he could break in a half-second.

In just this same way is the son of God trained by the world into believing he is powerless.

HE DOETH THE WORKS

Here comes the day—fresh, moving, ripe with promise and plans. One thing is sure: despite our finest efforts, our grandest hopes, we all know unexpecteds will jump headfirst into our moments and demand resolution.

So how do we do our doings?

Wait—perhaps the better question is: who is doing our doings? Is it us, with our minuscule skills and savvy, our finite prejudices and pains?

Or is it the one Self, expressing effortlessly through our listening ear? Or is it both—sometimes One, sometimes me?

Speaking for myself, the answer is both. (Those of you who hear only the One and no other can fold up this letter now; you need no reminders from anyone.)

But for the rest of us, let's take a moment to recall the difference between these two movements.

A peaceful and authentic doing is the one in which we act, not from our own limited under-standing (so often skewed toward littleness), but from that bidding which comes to us from the one Mind. And let us be clear about the bidding. Despite its flawlessness, despite its exquisite fiber, it cannot reach, ever, a cluttered and inflexible mind. Only the mind that has given way to stillness can hear the subtle whisper of the Unseen.

That is why we meditate, why we keep faithful to the daily work; why, hour after hour, we place ourselves under the discipline of silent listening. In surrendering to Silence, we are offering ourselves as empty vessels, willing to be His hands. We are cleaning away the one barrier to receiving: human graffiti.

Please remember—listening to the Silence makes no sense at all to those who operate solely from human intelligence. Be private about it; it will keep your practice unpolluted, and it will spare you needless hurt. Only One need know you are surrendering.

And here is the great blessing—One is all you need.

ꗛ ꗜ

"There is in all things an inexhaustible sweetness and purity; a silence that is a fount of action and joy. It rises up in wordless gentleness and flows out to me from the unseen roots of all created being ..."

—Thomas Merton

THERE'S WILLING TO RECEIVE, AND THEN THERE'S REALLY WILLING TO RECEIVE

Somewhere in a town much like yours and mine, there were two seekers who were both longing for divine Grace. Like many others, they had often heard about a certain sacred fountain which reportedly was filled with divine waters. The fountain was located in a city many miles away (isn't it always?), but despite the distance, both men were determined to journey there and drink the waters.

And so they did. One traveled just as he was, carrying only a water bottle slung around his waist. His companion, who was somewhat more cautious, brought along a knapsack filled with food, clothes, and a small brass cup.

After weeks of grueling travel, the two finally arrived at the sacred fountain; and just as everyone had said, it was streaming forth clear, sparking waters. Elated, both men immediately reached into the fountain to get their fill. But no sooner had the first one filled his brass cup to the brim, than he noticed that his companion was able to scoop up an entire bottleful. More Grace for his friend! He felt bitterly deprived.

"Look at this!" he said. "How unfair! Here we both traveled the same distance, endured the same hardships, climbed over the same tough rocks, and yet you have a full bottle of Grace, while I have only a small cup! Haven't I earned just as much? Frankly, I can only conclude that God is unjust!"

"But what has God to do with it?" asked his friend. "Look here—the fountain is full to bursting! Clearly, God's grace is the same for all. It is you who chose to keep only a cupful of space open for His gift."

LAUGHING ALL THE WAY

According to one Zen master, our first glimpses of Truth are Aha! moments. Later on, realizations become *Hahahaha!* The cosmic laugh.

And why does the *Hahahaha!* response take longer to emerge? Because until our identity has shifted truly and inwardly from the small self to the one Self, most stuff doesn't seem funny. How can it? The small, finite self sees everything from small, finite eyes, and thus all of its perceptions are mistaken ones. And departing from this narrow, separated way of seeing rarely happens overnight; in most of our cases it takes time, persistence, and plain hard work.

But the hard work does yield results. So one way to observe where you are on heaven's map is to notice how long it takes for you to chuckle over your dramas. And we don't mean nervous laughter—we're talking about a rich, inner, warm, bubble of feeling towards whatever crisis appears to be going on. It's a smile that is gut deep, sourced by an inner trust that goodness is the core substance of all Life. And that depth of trust develops only from years of devoted spiritual practice. Without the practice, our trust tends to be shallow and quick to crumble in the face of tough, gritty appearances.

One other thing: that divine *Hahahaha* is not a feeling we can force, or install like some magnificent new showerhead. Not now, not ever. It is a spontaneous response that expresses Itself from within—after we've done the work, and done the work, and done the work all over again. We carry on, noticing (without judgment) when we're caught by depression or fear or anger or ennui, all the while working on surrendering the illusory self from which dark feelings arise.

Then, out of the blue, the unearthly *Hahahaha!* begins to show Itself—at the oddest moments. With me, it sometimes occurs when I'm working on an appearance. I will be sitting, still as glass, listening, sunk in the silence as deep as I can go. And there It is, this absolutely inappropriate and outrageous tickle on the inside, erupting into a smile which simply paints itself across my face without warning.

Does it happen all the time? Not for me. Not yet. But it does happen, and each time it occurs, my faith deepens imperceptibly; my sense of the Eternal Smile gets stronger and more sure. In other words, I become less me. More I. And you know how I feel about that.

Hahahaha!

HOPPER'S DISCOVERY

Maybe you've known someone like Hugh Hopper; most of us have. He was a perfectly reasonable fellow who lived a perfectly reasonable life doing perfectly reasonable things, coping with perfectly reasonable problems and enjoying perfectly reasonable rewards. In fact, there was only one thing about Hopper that was not perfectly reasonable—he was not happy.

Well, so what, you may say. Who is? And that's exactly what Hopper said to himself for more years than he could count. But the divine Spirit, as we all know, can be as irksome as a young child asking for a new toy and just as persistent. And this bothersome Spirit kept after Hopper like a bad itch, asking him over and over and over: where's happiness?

Eventually, the day came when Hopper said to himself: I've got to find out! And feeling just a little nervous, he said goodbye to all his friends and went off to find someone who could answer his question.

It's a tough question, of course. There's no point in kidding about a thing like that. We all know it's tough. So Hopper traveled through many cities, many towns, many countries, looking for one who knew All. He ran into many who knew some, but some wasn't what he wanted. He wanted All. Thus he continued to travel. And along the way, he noticed his habits were beginning to change, ever so subtly. He wore simpler clothing, because it was easier to walk that way. He carried only one little sack, because it didn't weigh him down. He ate sparsely, because sparsely was just about all he could afford. He slept in modest rooms, because they were less bother. And he talked less, because most of the time he was busy pondering.

In fact, pondering became his passion. Wherever he traveled, he kept asking himself: where's happiness? Then he would walk a while in silence, waiting to see if an answer came out of the blue, or wherever it is answers come from.

Years passed. And then one quiet morning Hopper suddenly appeared back in his home town. Of course, by now almost no one recognized him. He was thinner and grayer, and there was a curious stillness about him that made him seem almost, well, magical.

But changed or not, there was one old friend who did spot him. Peering out from his porch, the friend shouted, "Hopper, is that you?"

"Yes, it's me," said Hopper.

"Well, come on in for some tea!" said his friend. And sitting down over some steaming cups of tea and hot bread, they had a good chat. His friend said, "You know, Hopper, when you left here you were looking desperately for happiness, and now, I must say, you seem happy as a lark. Tell me—how did you manage to find it?"

"Well," said Hopper, "it's a funny thing. Turns out it was right here all along—as soon as I got rid of the fellow who was looking for it somewhere else."

DON'T COMPARE

Inside a pleasant summer garden, an ant and a butterfly were having an argument about which one was more valuable.

"I'm more beautiful," said the butterfly. "Anybody can see that."

"But I'm more industrious," replied the ant.

"I can fly," said the butterfly, making loops in the air. "Look."

"I can crawl," said the ant, waving multitudinous legs. "Really, really fast."

"I have two lives," said the butterfly.

"I can lift six times my weight in food," said the ant.

Just about then a ferocious wind whooshed into the garden and blew the ant, the butterfly, and all of the flowers right into oblivion. When the wind had finally calmed down, there was nothing left but a couple of rocks. One rock said to its neighbor:

"Boy, listening to those two got me all depressed. We can't do any of that stuff. Compared to them, we have absolutely no value at all!"

"Well, except for one little thing," replied the other rock serenely. "We're still here."

A Poem by Ella Wheeler Wilcox

God and I in space alone
and nobody else in view.
"And where are the people, O Lord," I said,
"the earth below, and the sky o'er head
and the dead whom once I knew?"

"That was a dream," God smiled and said,
"A dream that seemed to be true.
There were no people, living or dead,
there was no earth, and no sky o'er head;
there was only Myself—in you."

"Why do I feel no fear," I asked,
"meeting You here this way?
For I have sinned I know full well—
And is there heaven, and is there hell,
and is this the Judgment Day? "

"Nay, those were but dreams,"
the Great God said,
"Dreams that have ceased to be.
There are no such things as fear or sin,
there is no you—you never have been —
there is nothing at all
but Me."

CELL RENEWAL

Trees waved in the afternoon sun, and under the bobbing leaves sat two good monks, discussing the astonishing case of a celebrated nobleman who had recently fallen into disgrace. It was a particularly disturbing turn of events, because for years this man had inspired his countrymen with accomplishment after accomplishment. His fame had risen to exceptional heights, and his victories were stellar. Thus, to onlookers, his entire life seemed like an endless golden thread, upon which he walked in perfect balance.

Until the day when—without warning—this much-honored hero slipped and fell. In the blink of an eye, he somehow entangled himself in a wave of darkness, and from there he crashed straight down into the bowels of the earth.

Oh, the agony of sunken splendor! The hero was cast in prison, where his long, golden life now seemed like a remote and impossible dream.

All were shocked by his descent, including the two monks, who were deep in discussion about this tormented soul. One said, "And all this time we believed he was good. If only we had known of his evil tendencies, we could have spared ourselves this shock!"

"Yes," murmured the other, "that's the hardest thing—discovering that one we trusted and loved is evil."

A third monk overheard the discussion and said, "Evil! Why do you call him evil? His action was a mistake, for which he must pay a price, but surely we cannot define anyone totally by either his good actions or his cruel ones."

"Why, Brother!" exclaimed the second monk. "If not by his actions, then how can we define him?"

The third monk replied, "As a window, like yourself, which is capable of being closed and dark in one moment or open and radiant in another."

"What!" the second monk exclaimed. "Are you saying you feel pity for this man and wish him to be sent away from prison?"

"Why, no!" said the third monk. "Prison may well be his release."

"Release? Prison?" cried the two monks. "How can that be?"

"It is in the quiet of his cell," said the third monk, "that this man may at long last be free to examine his real jailer—himself.

"Consider," he continued, "once he has sufficient time to examine his mistake, he may begin to realize the truth that he is the window, and not the storm. Of course, as soon as he comprehends that, he is on the road to becoming his true Self."

"His true Self?" said the first monk. "Do you mean the great hero he was before the tragedy?

"Ah, no." said the third monk. "Believing he was a great hero was his greatest block to awakening. But look! Now that block has been blown to bits, so the way is open for him to see who he is."

"Then are you saying that this man's fall was planned by God?" asked the first monk.

The third monk shook his head. "God, a policeman?" he chuckled. "Never! God neither plans nor executes our falls. But," he said, offering them a broad smile, "He sure uses them."

DECIDING THE TRUTH IS TRUE

Years and years ago—out of the blue—there emerged one lone and wild-eyed visionary who decided to challenge the popular world-is-flat theory. Probably there were others before him who had pondered this notion and questioned it. But this fellow did more than have a suspicion. Much more. In fact, he did the unthinkable—he tested it.

Just for a moment, put yourself in his place. Imagine what he went through during the process, as he struggled to prove outwardly what he *knew* within.

It could not have been an easy process. For no matter how sure he was that the earth was round, you know his mind must have pestered him with doubts—because that's what a mind does: pester, annoy, distract, mislead. And it does the job beautifully.

What if he were wrong?

What if everyone else were right?

What if, after all, the world were flat as a stone-ground pancake? And what if, when his ship came to the edge, it pitched over abruptly into the abyss?

Nevertheless, at some one soul-stopping moment, this brave soul came to a decision to proceed as if the Truth were true.

Despite all warnings from friends and family, despite prevailing opinion, despite appearances of doom, despite his own personal doubts, despite wind, hail, and storm—our friend took a long, deep breath and placed his trust full-strength on his deep inner intuition. And he set sail.

What about you?

Are you living in a flat universe?

Or are you setting sail on Truth?

It's not easy. Using a larger-than-life lens never is. You'll face a long, hard wall of limited beliefs. (Whose? Yours.) So it comes down to this: despite prevailing opinion, despite fears, despite doubts, despite habits, despite delusions large and small—do we have the courage to pin our faith on He who is here but unseen?

It's a choice we have to make every day, every hour. Actually, every minute. Either we listen and nod and dance to the graffiti of human belief, or we make the decision to place our trust Godward. And it does take guts! But we can do it. We must do it—forsake the external cues and turn instead to our inner Voice, letting It guide us safely through the sea of life, come hell or high water.

Do it.

Call on Him.

Reaching in for His still small voice is the only way we come to experience that the world is not flat. That Love *is* real. That Peace *is* present. That Life *is* joy.

And that we and God are not two.

THOU ART

This world is nothing
but a dance of shadows,
a line drawn between
darkness and light,
joy and oppression,
time and eternity.
Learn to read this subtle line,
for it tells all the secrets of creation.
Although you may not know it,
if you love anyone, it is Him you love;
if you turn your head in any direction,
it is toward Him you turn.
Let go of everything,
completely lose yourself on this path,
then your every doubt will be dispelled.
With absolute conviction, you'll cry out—
I am God!
I am the One I have found!
In the light I praised You
and never knew it.
In the dark I slept with you
and never knew it.
I always thought that I was me,
but no, I was You and never knew it.

—Fakhruddin Araqi

YOU ARE WHAT YOU SEEK

All the Buddhas and all sentient beings are nothing but the Universal Mind, besides which nothing exists. This Mind which has always existed is unborn and indestructible. It is not green or yellow, and has neither form nor appearance. It does not belong to the categories of things that exist or do not exist, nor can It be reckoned as being new or old. It is neither long nor short, big nor small, for It transcends all limits, measures, names, speech and every method of treating It concretely. ...

The Universal Mind alone is the Buddha, and there is no distinction between the Buddha and sentient beings, except that sentient beings are attached to forms and so seek externally for Buddhahood. By their very seeking for It they lose It. ... If they could only put a stop to their conceptual thoughts, they would realize that the Buddha is directly before them.

—Huang Po

PARADOX

Without going
out the door
one can know
the whole world;

Without glancing
out the window
one can see
the Way of heaven.

The further one goes
the less one knows.

Thus the Sage does not go,
yet he knows;
He does not look,
yet he sees;
He does not do,
yet all is done.

—Tao Te Ching

DREAMING

Imagine a child sleeping next to its parents and dreaming it is being beaten or is painfully sick. The parents cannot help the child, no matter how much it suffers.

If the child could awaken itself, it could be freed of this suffering automatically. In the same way, one who realizes that his own Mind is Buddha frees himself instantly from sufferings arising from the ceaseless change of birth-and-death. If a Buddha could prevent it, do you think he would allow even one sentient being to fall into hell?

What is obstructing realization? Nothing but your own half-hearted desire for truth. Think of this and exert yourself to the utmost.

—Bassui Zenji

FREE!

On his way to church, a scholar was surprised to see a man in tattered clothes and barefoot. Nevertheless, as a good Christian, he greeted the poor man, "May God give you a good morning!"

The poor man replied cheerfully, "I have never yet had a bad morning."

"Then may God give you good luck!"

"I have never yet had bad luck."

"Well, may God give you happiness!"

"I have never yet been unhappy."

The scholar then asked the man, "Could you please explain yourself to me? I do not understand."

And the poor man replied, "With pleasure! You wish me a good morning, yet I have never had a bad morning. For when I am hungry, I praise God; when I feel cold, when it is raining or snowing, I praise God; and that is why I have never had a bad morning.

"You wish that God may give me luck; however, I have never had bad luck. This is because I live with God and always feel what He does for me is for the best. Whatever God sends me, be it pleasant or unpleasant, I accept with a grateful heart. That is why I have never had bad luck.

"Finally, you wish that God should make me happy. But I have never been unhappy. For all I desire is to follow God's will; I have surrendered my will so totally to God's will that whatever God wants, that is what I also want.

"That is why I have never been unhappy."

—Meister Eckhart

LOOKING THROUGH A GLASS LIGHTLY

Have you noticed how subtly and silently God's hand can move? It can be quieter than a snowflake. When a challenge is before me, I may work and work and pray and pray for days or weeks—or longer—with no perceptible change in the structure of the challenge. But time is a zero in the eye of God, and if I remain true to Truth and continue to ask for the nature of God to reveal itself, there comes a moment when things are no longer the way they were. They are a new way instead. A cloud which was heavy and compelling is gone in the blink of an eye. A difficulty which had shape and form and dramatic color is suddenly quite gone. A pain which had no end suddenly has no beginning or reality at all. This morning, here was all this stuff.

And now—there it isn't.

What it takes, first, is a change in my own perception. I have to pack up and put away the concept that is blocking the flow of God. Often it is difficult to notice how tightly chained we are to a belief, because the lock is occurring on a level below our awareness. If we observe, though, that the fruits of a belief are recurring in our life, we can safely deduce that a belief is in operation and then place it up on the table for healing.

For example, I went through a period when I felt responsible about a failure in business and must have believed I deserved to suffer, because a number of painful events began to parade before me, one by one.

I prayed often to see God in this situation, to catch hold of the truth that there is no failure in heaven. But I will tell you frankly it was not until I began to realize, despite my own judgments, that I was forever one with God and deserved to feel His happiness, that the clouds began to stealthily disappear. I say stealthily, because often they had disappeared for some time before I even noticed their absence. The fact was, a healing occurred only after I managed to drop my own belief in the concept of failure—to forgive myself.

Some call it purification. And so it is. Normally, of course, we speak of purification as healing bad habits. But it is much more than that. Essentially, purification is the willingness to shed those concepts that keep us identified with littleness. Our commonly shared human beliefs form a dreadful barrier in our lives, for they lead to an entire network of terrors which arise from the human notion of separation. We are not clean until we have begun to dis-identify from this deep, dark notion and the great quantities of guilt that it spawns.

In my experience, there are two necessary steps in moving toward Freedom. One step, the crucial one, is to allow Silence to inform us that we are Spirit, children of God. Until we begin to grasp that, we are nowhere. And the other step is to begin paying exquisite attention to each appearance before us—in other words, to monitor our life fabric for the symptoms of limiting beliefs. When we spot one, we tweeze it out by watching it without judgment. Judgment-free watching requires a sea of patience, but it works.

It works because it cleanses, and one day we arise and discover (without fanfare or fuss) that where there once was littleness, now there is Love.

From The Cloud of Unknowing

Lift up your heart to God with a meek stirring of love; and intend God Himself and none of His created things. And be sure not to think of anything but Himself so that nothing may work in your mind or in your will but only Himself. And do whatever you can to forget all the creatures that God ever made and all their works.

When you first begin, you find just a darkness and, as it were, a cloud of unknowing—you do not know what—except that you feel in your will a naked intent toward God. This darkness and this cloud, no matter what you do, is between you and your God, and hinders you, so that you can neither see Him clearly by the light of understanding in your reason, nor feel Him in the sweetness of love in your affection. Therefore, prepare to abide in this darkness as long as you must, evermore crying after Him whom you love. For if ever you are to see Him or feel Him in this life, it must always be in this cloud and in this darkness.

But now you ask me, "How shall I think upon God Himself, and what is He?" To this I cannot answer you, except to say, "I don't know." For with your question you have brought me into that same darkness and into that same cloud of unknowing that I want you to be in. For of all other creatures and their works—yes, and of the works of God Himself—a man may, through Grace, have fullness of knowing, and he can well think upon them; but upon God Himself, no man can think.

And therefore I wish to leave everything I can think, and choose for my love that thing which I cannot think, because He may well be loved, but not thought. By love, He may be gotten and held; but by thinking—never.

IT'S NOT BECOMING; IT'S BE HERE

Let's talk about everyday-bread-and-butter prayers.

Mind you, we're not discussing High Prayer here. As you know, High Prayer takes place at a level of consciousness in which the only realization necessary is "God is." It's a vast, wordless, and gorgeous prayer. And in fact, it's the only one you'll ever need.

But to be blunt, few of us remain consistently at that elegant level of awareness. There are countless moments in which, in the face of specific traumas, a particularized prayer feels more comforting and helpful. So let's talk about that kind.

Think about it; two groups of cells get together for coffee one morning in a petri dish and discuss projects at hand. Group one, whom we'll call the Ted Cells, announce they've been told to alert themselves to a possible promotion at work. The Ted Cells are very excited about this information; they claim the entire Ted organism is now readying itself for this dazzling future promotion.

Group two, whom we'll call the Sam Cells, congratulate the other group on their new assignment and then say they, too, have a new project — they've actually been promoted at work. Right at this very moment, they say, their organism is busying itself to accommodate its brand new status.

And from whom are these cell groups taking their orders? Ted and Sam. Here's Ted, who urgently wants a more challenging job and is praying that someday soon he will be promoted. And here's Sam, who urgently wants a more challenging job. Sam is thanking God for answering his prayer.

Now, what are we saying? Are we claiming that somewhere there is a God who thinks, "Hey, I like Sam's prayer better; I'm going to make his dream come true"? You know we're not saying that. God isn't even remotely conscious of job titles or pay schedules or mortgage payments. Only we bother ourselves about such small (and finite) potatoes. God is a split-second and endless Living-hood.

What God is conscious of, in this case, is that the Mind of Sam has a door open for divine activity. Why? Because he hasn't paralyzed his prayer by requesting that it come true tomorrow — that endearing and imaginary date whose primary claim to fame is that it never, ever arrives.

Sam gave his prayer legs to move by accepting good the moment he asked for it. Sure enough, he gets the new job. Ted, on the other hand, has told his Inner Self that he wants something wonderful to almost happen—but not quite.

So for Ted something wonderful almost happens. But not quite.

And haven't you made this mistake in your prayers? I sure have. I spent years making it, over and over again. It's an innocent mistake. There you are, praying with an open heart and earnest good will, and you neglect to notice that the tone of your prayer is one of complete doubt about its fulfillment. You get still, you cleanse your mind, you do all the right and pure pre-prayer movements, and then you say, "Oh, please, let me experience Divine Love tomorrow, soon, someday! Let me experience this sometime other than now."

Well, the Divine is nothing if not a good sport. It ponders mightily over what "not now" means, but try as It might, It can find no answer. So It tunes in again, and there you are, saying, "Oh, please make everything well soon. Because darn!—everything's a mess right now." And finally the boundless, timeless, ever-alive Divine says, "Okey- dokey."

JUST DIG

Remember, it is the Hidden Power within us that pulls the strings; there lies the guiding force, there is the life; there, one might say, is the man himself. Never think of yourself as a mere body with its various appendages. The body is like the axe of a carpenter—dare we think the axe to be the carpenter himself? Without this Inner Cause, which dictates both action and inaction, the body is of no more use than the weaver's shuttle without a weaver, the writer's pen without a writer, or the coachman's whip without a horse and carriage.

Honor the highest thing in the Universe; it is the power on which all things depend; it is the light by which all life is guided.

Dig within. Within is the wellspring of Good; and it is always ready to bubble up—if you just dig.

—Marcus Aurelius

BE A SONG FOR CHRISTMAS

You are a song.

You are an exquisite, perfect melody. Your melody and my melody and the melodies of all mankind form a concerto so exquisite you have never heard anything like it. Divine music.

The trouble is, we can't hear it when our mind is busy with its ordinary run of thoughts. Sounds of this order are subtler than snowflakes. They become apparent only after we surrender all of our meager, superfluous sounds and let them disappear like wavelets into silence. Then come the first, faint strains of the music within; and it is not just we ourselves who are caught by its magic.

Others, not even knowing why, will find themselves responding to its sheer beneficence. And yet none of this music is the kind that can be heard by human ears; it is more like a series of vibrations read by the soul, a divine current. However it feels to us, its theme is ever the same—wholeness.

Now, I know that until inner discipline has taken hold, it often appears easier to reach for happiness from "out there." How well I know! It seems so easy, so fast, so available—a sugarplum here, a delicacy there—but the fact is, sugarplums and delicacies melt away.

Inner music is accessible forever.

So find a chair, move into it, close your eyes. It's Christmas, and you deserve the finest of all gifts—Yourself.

Close your eyes, listen to your breath, and let your thoughts drift where they will. Wait for stillness to settle in; it will tiptoe in on its soft feet, I promise. And now listen for the music, the "Center-sound," the You of you singing Its own private song.

Think of it! The song inside is more than a pretty tune—it is a healing force. When you have reached the depth of Quiet that allows your song to reveal itself, it will not only bless you, but bless every brother and sister you have ever met.

In fact, it will bless every brother and sister you haven't met. It will bless every brother and sister there is; bless every brother and sister that ever was; bless every brother and sister there ever will be.

It will bless the One.

RIGHT HERE

Look to this day!
For it is life, the very life of life.
In its brief course
lie all the verities and realities
of your existence.
For yesterday
is already a dream
and tomorrow
is only a vision;
but today, well lived,
makes every yesterday
a dream of happiness,
and every tomorrow
a vision of hope.
—from the Sanskrit

Divine Sense

The act of seeing,
though not what you see,
is what you are looking for.

The act of hearing,
though not what you hear,
is what you are listening for.

The act of touching,
though not what you touch,
is what you are reaching for.

The act of tasting,
though not what you taste,
is what nourishes you.

The act of smelling,
though not what you smell,
is the breath of life.

—Bruce Becker

SUMMING UP

Heaven does nothing:
its non-doing is its serenity.
Earth does nothing:
its non-doing is its rest.

From the union of these two non-doings
all actions proceed,
all things are made.
How vast, how invisible
this coming-to-be!
All things come from nowhere!
How vast, how invisible—
no way to explain it!
All beings in their perfection are
born of non-doing.
Hence it is said,
"Heaven and earth do nothing
yet there is nothing they do not do."

Where is the man
who can attain to this non-doing?
—Chuang Tzu, 500 B.C.

SILENCE

The inner silence is self-surrender. And that is living without the sense of ego.

Solitude is in the mind of man. One might be in the thick of the world and yet maintain perfect serenity of mind; such a person is always in solitude. Another may stay in the forest, but still be unable to control his mind. He cannot be said to be in solitude.

Solitude is an attitude of the mind. A man attached to the things of life cannot get solitude, wherever he may be. A detached man is always in solitude.

There is a state of meditation which transcends speech and thought; this deep meditation is eternal speech. Silence is ever speaking; it is the perennial flow of a wordless language. In fact, it is interrupted by speaking; for words obstruct this mute language.

Lectures may entertain individuals for hours without improving them. Silence, on the other hand, is permanent and benefits the whole of humanity. Silence is unceasing eloquence. It is living language. This is the state when words cease and silence prevails.

—Ramana Maharshi

Reloading the Hard Disk

The other day I was reviewing a mistake that got made. As it happens, I was the one who made it.

Here's what I noticed: It's very difficult to forgive yourself for mistakes. For one thing, you're supposed to know better. For another thing, you're supposed to know better. And thirdly, you're supposed to know better.

So it's tough to extend tenderness towards oneself under such circumstances; one has to face the awful fact that the ego still has its fingers on one's behavior.

By the ego, I mean the part of my mind and your mind that lives in fear and thus responds with fear to almost anything that happens — if we're not watching. In this case, I wasn't watching.

Now, I don't mean to say the ego is evil; it's not. It is simply an energy that lives scared, and so you have to pay attention to its movements. Because whatever lives scared tends to live mean.

In fact, if the ego were our only resource, we would be in serious trouble. Luckily, it's not. All of us who have tumbled onto the Self beyond the ego are aware we have a major Friend in our corner; one who rescues us again and again and again from our self-made tangles.

Of course, the Friend can't transfer Its wisdom outright; It can only point to our mistakes.

It's like a child learning to tie his shoelace.

Before he gets the hang of it, he's going to tie it the wrong way 50 times, 100 times, maybe even 5000 times. And we're the friend, saying patiently, "No, that's not quite the way it goes. Watch. *Now try it again*."

In the beginning, while the child is trying to copy movements he does not understand, he will do it wrong over and over and over and over. And get frustrated. And get mad. And kick off the shoe and call it a toad.

But as he proceeds to tie it wrong over and over and over again, something in his mind begins to quietly open. Eventually, in one breathless moment, he will grasp the principle of the knot.

Then he's free.

He won't need you now; he's off tying bows in shoelaces, string, hair-bows, telephone cords, ribbon, wrapping cord—anything long and thin that can bend.

He doesn't need you, because the principle of tying is embedded in his computer. It's installed. Now he can use it; now it's up and running and rushing into high action on its own.

So you know when I tell you that somebody made a mistake yesterday and it was me, that the principle of Oneness isn't yet fully installed on my hard disk.

But here's something I'm certain of—*It will be.*

METAPHYSICAL HEALING

Let it be clear to you that the personal self cannot heal, teach, or govern harmoniously. It must be held in abeyance in order that the Christ may have full dominion within our consciousness.

The work that is done with the letter of truth, with declarations and so-called treatments, is insignificant compared with what is accomplished when we have surrendered our will and action to the Christ.

The Christ comes to our consciousness most clearly in those moments when we come face to face with problems for which we have no answer and no power with which to surmount them, and we realize that 'I can of mine own self do nothing.' In these moments of self-effacement, the gentle Christ overshadows us, permeates our consciousness, and brings the 'peace, be still' to the troubled mind.

—*The Infinite Way* by Joel Goldsmith

JOLT MANAGEMENT

I was walking over to the grocery store the other day, wearing my favorite jacket (which by now is severely shape-challenged), carrying a tote bag over one arm. Suddenly a carload of teenagers appeared, like misdirected lightning, and hurled their vehicle around a corner. They missed swiping three pedestrians by a hair. A thin hair.

I jumped. The suddenness of it threw me into an unsettled place, and I began walking over-carefully, as though I were sidestepping broken glass. By the time I arrived at the store I was in a serious fret. My mind was chattering—always a bad sign.

So I needed to re-center. There was a friendly little delicatessen planted right next to the grocery. I went inside the deli; immediately I was engulfed in that delicious aroma common to all delis everywhere: spiced meats, cheeses, garlic, tomato sauce, creative pastas. You know, food cooked the way you wish mom had cooked it.

There was a huge, eclectic beverage freezer in back; I pulled out a mainstream soda and took it over to a table. Sat down, drank some soda, inhaled the glorious essence of deli. I thought about how much fun it is to be a teenager, full of vim and vitamins and ready to attempt spirited speeds in your car.

A moment or two later, I began to see they meant no harm, that car full of youngsters; they were simply trying out one of the planet's toys with sixteen-year-old abandon. Their energy scared a few of us; it hurt no one.

As I thought about the way minds work when they are in teen mode and recalled the years I had worn that very same mindset, I began to relax. Not long after, I even began to start smiling over the entire incident.

The deli owner saw me grinning and asked me why I looked so happy. I told him the soda had turned out to be especially nourishing and then inquired if he had some fresh sliced turkey. He did. I bought it. It was fabulicious.

On the way home, no car swooshed by me at a dizzying pace, but if it had, I would have been ready. I would have stepped back, paused, and hurtled a pound of peace after it.

Fair's fair.

Making "Misteaks"

This topic is not exactly a remote one. Far from it. I've backslid so many times I have scrape marks up and down the length of my spine. But then, I'm a hard nut to crack. You probably don't make all the blunders I do. In my case, mistakes are like vitamins—I make three a day whether I need them or not.

So, onwards about backsliding. By backsliding I mean all those occasions during the day when I have a choice of responding from my heart or from my ego, and I choose the ego. I do that because, for a brief moment, I'm under the illusion it feels better.

For example. The other day I overheard someone at work belittling a fellow colleague, an action that would cause any decent person to wince. Well, I'm decent enough, and I winced.

Of course, wincing itself isn't backsliding. Wincing is wincing—there's no black marks here. I suspect that even angels wince on occasion. There's probably a Grouse Bar & Grill you can visit up there, a lovely, quiet place where you sip ginseng beer and compare ouches. No, wincing isn't backsliding.

Here's what backsliding is: carrying that wince into your mind, planting it in a pot, watering it, tending to it, encouraging it to sprout and grow little green things out of the soil. And then proudly placing the plant on a windowsill and watching it grow into a thigh-high grudge.

I've done that, and even managed to reassure myself it was appropriate behavior while I was doing it. Why? Well, there's a curious little kink in our mind that allows us to feel superior when we are busy judging someone else.

So condemnation is a very tempting pot of glue to step into, and once you're inside, it's hard to exit. If you're familiar with the properties of glue, you know why.

At one point I noticed I was doing this, growing my scant wince into an enormous new species of Chrysanthemum leucanthemum. And in a moment of sanity I decided to nip it in the bud. (Am I terrific, or what?)

I trashed the plant, pot and all, and sat down to rethink. This time, rather than focusing on the less-than-luminous behavior of the colleague in question, I took a look at why she might have done it.

When I did, it occurred to me that only frightened people belittle others. So here I was, carrying a loaded judgment about a person who was too insecure, at one particular moment, to act in a larger way.

Does that mean it's OK for people who are scared to act in an incendiary manner? No. It doesn't even mean we can't say something to the person who has made this kind of mistake. In fact, honest feedback often helps people grow. What it does mean, though, is that I am not assigned the luxury of growing grudges; my job is to see the person's fear and work with that.

In this case, as I looked straight into the fear which had evoked this person's insensitivity, I lost all interest in the grudge and tossed it in the garbage for keeps. From there, my interest in the entire event seemed to dissipate into nothing. Another way to say it would be that after I had seen the situation clearly, I simply forgave it. Once forgiven, it disappears.

So what we're after, if we want to awaken, is to fully release the situation until it melts out of our mind like old snow. Then we're back on the road again, light as air, no weights on our windowsill, no cords binding us down to lead-heavy thoughts of rebuke.

Traveling light—there's no feeling quite like it.

ON THANKSGIVING

Thanksgiving Day is a celebration of freedom. When we give thanks to someone, we are saying, "I am grateful for the benefit I have received from you." The benefit can take the form of food, shelter, clothing, health, wealth, opportunity, understanding, companionship, etc. Always our thanksgiving is for some greater sense of freedom that we are experiencing in ourselves. We are grateful to and give thanks for anything that helps us to break through (or approach breaking through) the sense of limitation or bondage in ourselves. To the degree that we are being lifted out of our bondage, to that degree are we thankful and ready to give thanks to whomever or whatever is bringing about the experience of freedom.

Thanksgiving Day is a holiday set apart to give thanks to God, and if we are to understand the meaning of this special day, we must first understand this God to whom we give thanks. Most major religions today have only one God; they may each have different names for God, but there is only one God.

The most common definition of God is Omnipresence, Omnipotence, and Omniscience, which is all presence, all power, and all knowledge. Because it is not possible to comprehend or conceptualize Omnipresence, Omnipotence, and Omniscience, in giving thanks to God we are giving thanks to something that is beyond our understanding.

This limited understanding defines the bondage we experience. Since God is All-in-all—there being nothing beyond all power, all presence, and all knowledge—any greater understanding or awareness of God is a greater sense of freedom. Because this greater sense of freedom can only come from God, we give our thanks to God for the gift He/She/It bestows upon us. In this case, a particular day has been set aside, Thanksgiving Day, in which to say, "Thank You, God."

—Bruce Becker

EVERYTHING'S RELATIVE

Recently I had lunch with a friend who was having great difficulty with her mother. Each visit home seemed to trigger odd bouts of unkindness; her mother would become angry at the drop of a hat and start shouting over nothing.

My friend is a kind person, yet she was weary from these encounters. It is hard to walk gracefully in such treacherous territory, she said. Most of all, she was sad that her spiritual practice did not seem to protect her from the vagaries of human temper.

I said yes, that was a tough one. Troubled relationships are one of the hardest lessons we ever face.

It seems so personal, after all! It is one thing to accept unruly acquaintances and strangers whose bodies dance by us only rarely. It is quite another to accept the disturbances that issue from our own immediate circle. To imagine we can brush unkindnesses away lightly is unrealistic; most of us have hidden expectations toward our friends and families, and it hurts when they go unmet.

A mother, for example, was destined to love us. If for one reason or another she cannot do that, it might be smart to accept that and let it be so. But typically, our own primal needs interfere with such acceptance; we may go for years wishing silently for nurturing from the withholding parent, without even noticing we have such a hope in tow.

We don't notice the hope, because to our friends we are saying, with grownup common sense, "That's the way she is. I expect nothing more." But our cells are not in agreement; and so we visit the parent, wearing our adult reasoning on top and our primitive yearning underneath. This results in a split mind; no peace can ever come from such a state.

So what do we do when we find ourselves caught in a web of dislike? I mean, besides scream.

For one thing, we look with gentleness on our own response and allow it to be there. No forgiveness of another is possible if we are snarling at our own human reactions. Thoughts along the lines of, "You shouldn't be feeling this way!" are ludicrous and lead to a dead-end street. I know that, because I've had thousands of such thoughts, and trust me, they aren't worth the electrolytes they travel on.

What I can do, though, is intercept my own train of thought. When I notice I am feeling hurt or victimized and place those thoughts on a screen to give them breathing space, they immediately begin to grow smaller. For one thing, I can see where they come from—old longings; and I can see where they lead—more pain. The more I observe the thoughts and see their mechanical origins, the less power they retain. Eventually, they dissipate and deflate like stabbed balloons. Why? No resistance.

When mayors light firecrackers and shoot them up into the sky, we know there will be explosion sounds. We are prepared; they are not personal, there is no alarm when they actually burst into noise. We accept the noise and enjoy the dazzle of light.

So with my friend's mother—and we all have a relative like my friend's mother—we can work to disarm ourselves, accept the noise and enjoy the dazzle of light. All beings have something miraculous about them. It may be the way they cook pound cake; it may be their canniness with stocks; it may be the way they laugh—in large, loopy dollops of hilarity. It may be their grumpiness, which can seem almost comical. Or it may be that someone is a miracle because the freckles on their face are arranged with awesome precision.

It doesn't matter.

What matters is letting it be; learning how to let things be awful and love them anyway. And I promise you, we can do it. We are miracles, you and I.

WHAT YOU SEE IS WHAT YOU GET

Worries are like phantom flies
that buzz and flit before our eyes;
no matter how immense they feel,
the truth is that they are not real.
(And that's why no one ever got 'em
by running all around to swat 'em.)

There is no mischief flies can do,
unless we give them power to.
So when one flits beneath your nose,
and you are tempted to suppose
it's absolutely, really there—
that's the time to pause for prayer.
Despite how loud and long its buzz,
prayer will prove it never was.
And you'll find out before you're through,
the fly is no more there than "you."

No, flies don't cause our misery—
it's our belief in a private "me."
For only a separate self can seem
to see real substance in a dream.
And till you question what you fear,
You'll see a lot of flies out here.
For sadly, nothing can undo
beliefs that dwell unchecked in you.

God is always Here, and yet —
What we see is what we get.

Yes, flies are fake,
but they won't cease —
until we turn our mind to Peace.
So when you rest within the I,
pray for the mind that sees the fly —
for once the separate mind is free,
heaven is all it will ever see.

CLEANING UP

I took on a truly difficult adventure the other day—cleaning out a closet.

It was one of those overstuffed closets (nearly every life has one) packed with useless objects and clothing units which for one reason or another seem too historical or potentially viable to discard. Coats with life still in them; never-worn hats in search of an authentic event to attend; a bowed-but-unbroken suitcase; boxes of paper, books, shoes, boots, belts, questionable mufflers, odd bits of ribbon and elastic, magazines; old hairspray.

A recess flaunting its chaos; the kind of staggering mess which suggests that the road to order is way too long for any human to travel. On a normal day I would stare into this pocket of horror, and my heart would sink instantly into discouragement. Then I would sigh, close the door and walk away.

But one day something drove me to take up the closet's challenge—possibly it was the fact that the door was no longer able to close properly. In any event, I wasn't thrilled with my decision to cut through the fashion jungle, but having accepted the assignment, I moved forward with a certain courage. The closet was Everest and I was going to climb it. That was that.

My method was appallingly routine. I threw everything inside the closet out into the hall in two discrete piles. One would return to the closet, one would move on to the garbage. Bit by bit, handling one item at a time, I plodded through the wreckage until Garbage Pile A was impressively larger than Closet Pile B. (Of course, I tortured myself over several pieces along the way, weighing my attachment to the item against the sublime goal of simplicity.) Finally the closet was returned to its original nature—lean, neat housing for a few key fashion elements. The Garbage Pile I enclosed in plastic bags and deposited out back in a trash can.

This surgical process took several hours, and at the end I was worn out, a limp rag. I stood and stared at the newly elegant closet, applauded its spare look, and then sat down and had some coffee. At this point, it occurred to me how lovely it would be if one could do this same intensive housecleaning on ill-fitting relationships or uncomfortable jobs.

And of course, we can do this—it's just that it takes longer, and we're much more resistant about throwing away the stuff that keeps cluttering up our human situations—things like judgments, opinions, inertia, or wanting to be right forever and always. It's one thing to reluctantly toss out an old sweater, and it's quite another to say, "Well, I think I'll just accept her the way she is, even if she does appear cold and calculating." That requires relaxing a judgment, and if we've had that judgment on hand for a number of years, the reluctance to parting with it is enormous.

But every once in a while I bump into someone whose closet of opinions is lean and tidy and sparsely furnished. And what I notice is that these rare beings seem to live a happier life and that other people feel amazingly comfortable in their presence. Champions of low-maintenance living, these amazing souls have not only heard that less is more, but have incorporated that concept into their movements.

For example, I have a friend who is so relaxed and unfettered by judgment that even when insulted, he just chuckles. That's a rare art form — chuckling over insults. Whenever I see him, I wish the rest of us could adopt this man's amazingly wide scope of good humor. Clearly it would make our days brighter and our communications sweeter.

He's a treasure to know, because his interior closets are clean as a whistle. He can laugh at almost everything, brush away small annoyances like lint, sidestep explosions with elegance and charm, and forgive nearly everything. This leaves him free emotionally to employ major qualities like compassion, problem-solving, and humor.

I want my mind to look like that.

For Joel Goldsmith

by Charles, 1995

"He uttered his voice and the earth melted."
—Psalm 46:6

I traveled beyond the horizon,
I ventured beyond what we see;
Now I tell of the world eternal,
And the one Life behind you and me.

For hidden within the commotion
And the sound that drums in your ears,
There lies a peace and a stillness—
The Source of all that appears.

When the world around you grows heavy
And trouble looms large in your heart,
Take a moment to pause and to listen
To the Voice of which you are part.

For when the Silence is entered,
And when the Presence is felt,
Then in that moment He utters His voice,
And you will see the earth melt.

The world of seeming's a prison—
Let the work before us begin.
To open ourselves to the Presence
And set free the Splendor within.

MOLEHILLS

When I was nine, my brother whopped me in the mouth with a bag of marbles and killed one of my teeth.

We were arguing about something; I can't remember what. Probably how many goldfish can fit comfortably into a fishbowl. Or something else of equally intense importance. Whatever it was, it caused a temporary rip in our siblinghood.

The dead tooth got fixed up in pretty short order; today it's hard to tell anything ever happened. At family gatherings my brother and I get together and giggle about this and other high dramas from the past. He is a wonderful person; I bear him not one iota of ill will over the tooth killing; nor do I sustain any resentment over the fact that all of his teeth are still alive, while one of mine is deceased. It happened in the same way that Tuesday follows Monday, and that's that.

I mean—who cares?

Actually, I'm glad it happened. Because now, when my day gets whopped by a bag of marbles, I have personal reference material to remind me of how molehill these small traumas really are in the scheme of things. I'm not saying it works all the time; it doesn't. But it can prod me out of a too-personal view of things into a larger perspective.

There are other, similar devices one can use for this purpose; questions like: fifty years from now, will this matter? Essentially it does the same thing —sweeps the eye away from peering too closely at insignificant events.

And they are, by and large, insignificant. In any given tooth/marble confrontation, there's only that one moment when your mouth stings from the blow. Then the sting recedes, and you're left with two choices—A: make a big deal out of it, or B: forget about it.

Making a big deal out of it wins you attention, sympathy and lots of aftershock to work through. It's the attention part that often impels us to choose A—Sympathy! Warmth! Kind Words! You can see what it beckons to us, even when we have to pay a stiff price—wading knee deep in injured feelings for long, ruinous lengths of time.

B is a much smarter choice, of course, but since when have humans been famous for making the smarter choice?

Those who do, though, get a special prize. Forgetting about stuff wins you the freedom to move on to the next adventure and pay lower tolls on the road.

When the American space program first began sending humans into outer arenas of the universe, several astronauts reported that the trip had a tremendous impact on their mindset. One commented that when he first saw the earth from several million miles away, it literally stopped him cold.

He gazed down at the small blue sphere he called home, he said, and suddenly realized how pin-sized his house and fence and driveway and troubles were in comparison to the vastness of space. Apparently, this man has never been able to see things in quite the same way since. His brief glimpse of infinity forever altered his perception; he senses now that everyday troubles are, in fact, rather small particles of dust on the landscape of life.

One quick trip into outer space, and now he is a different person. Freer than he was before he saw the earth shrink into a blue dot.

He looks through a larger window now; he knows troubles will roll up his driveway and roll back down again. He is focused on the landscape and not the specks on the glass. He wears life with a slight grin, because he's fortunate enough to have seen the wide-angle shot—and it's gorgeous.

And it's called waking up.

My Life and Times
on Planet Looneybin

When you arrived here
did they tell you
the same thing they told me?
That you're a mortal body
and as fragile as a flea?
Did they warn you life was scary,
and you had to step with care?
Did they teach you we're all separate,
and that nothing's ever fair?

Did they say some folks are evil,
and should fill you full of dread?
And that an Act of God
could come along
and leave you deeply dead?
Did they say disease was normal
and you could expect your share?
Did they say God in His wisdom
placed the cold germ in the air?

Did they say you had to struggle?
And that working was real hard?
That life was like
a well-cooked steak:
—swell but slightly charred?
Did they say you had to be real kind,

yet be careful who you trust?
Love thy neighbor, sort of—
(with a soupcon of disgust)?

Did they say that marriage never works?
That Love can turn to Hate?
and when you got depressed by this—
did they tell you life was great?
Did they tell you God is mighty
and He pulled us from the void?
That He loves you—loves you ever so,
—except when He's annoyed?

Did they tell you suffering is divine
and to welcome every twinge?
Did they teach the ABCs of life—
Abhor, Beware and Cringe?
Did they say you are a sinner?
Did they tell you you're a fool?
And if you tried to question that—
did they keep you after school?

Ah, I see your teachers
were the same;
your head is just as full;
you heard the same old folderol;
you learned the same old bull.
Well, their words about this world
were right—
They spoke truth all along.

But the world, you see,
is just a dream—
so all they said is wrong!

Your job now is the same as mine—
to wipe your mind of lies.
And when that's done, the Truth Itself
leaps out like a Surprise.
Funny how it all turns out—
that our one and only sin
was falling for the myths we learned
on Planet Looneybin.

Q. Why Is It So Hard to Wake Up?
A. Who Is Asking the Question?

You know who is asking—the human mind. There are no questions in our Real Self. Many times over it has struck me that our search seems long, not because the Truth is so hidden, but because the ego doesn't really want the search to end.

My sense is that we find the kingdom as fast as we can stand it. And we can't stand it for a long time. After all, waking up isn't a matter of checking the mirror one morning and finding we're taller or younger or that our skin has cleared up. It's a burst of realization that the face in the mirror isn't Me. It's looking past the mirror, past the face—and being struck by the miracle of Consciousness Itself. Facelessness.

We call it a journey; but God is not waiting down the road apiece. He's Here. We're the ones who aren't Here; most often we're deep in Yesterdayville or Tomorrowland (two of our favorite amusement parks.) The instant we escape from there, we're Here.

It doesn't take time. Yes, it seems to, but here in our Human Hall of Mirrors lots of things seem to be what they're not. And time is one of our most cherished beliefs. For instance, when we start out, we all believe our spiritual practice will lead us to God. And of course, practice is vital. But it doesn't take us anywhere. It simply removes the blocks from our sight. Without blocks, *Is* is instantly visible.

Yes, some days it seems as though we are riddled with blocks, with concepts. "I am trapped in my own beliefs and cannot move!" we think. And in a spasm of despair, we surrender; simply let go and throw our mind open to God.

In that split second—without warning—comes the moment when we *see*. We see there is no brain, no second self, no time, no space, no other. Just as a separate scoop of ice cream left in the sun melts back into milkness, so our separate, personal self can disappear in a flash. And all that is left is what the separate self was so desperately hiding—I Am.

"I am looking for the face I had before the world was made."

—William Butler Yeats

LET'S EXAMINE THE POVERTY IN OUR MIND

Behold! In the world of time and space, an-other calendar starts its race—a brand spanking new January! Time to pause and take a long look at what notions are still gluing shut our Sight. Out there in the "universal mirror" we see multiple images of recession and lack, a clear signal we each need to examine, carefully, the beliefs we're wearing.

It's one thing to read in books that the sense of separation from God is our only cause of trouble; it's quite another to experience it at such depth that it triggers a flood of peace. And make no mistake—only the experience of peace has any power to it; toying with the idea of it is as empty as a popcorn box after a ballgame.

What's tricky about this practice is that faith-lessness often announces itself so subtly we barely notice it. Wincing as you pass by a homeless person, for instance, is a sure affirmation of the belief that he is separate from God. Worrying, fretting, doubting are all ploys our ego uses to lobby for the reality of good and evil. Yet these states seem like such an inherent part of us that we tend to let them hold sway without a thought. "Well, it's natural!" we say, "I can't help it."

Yes, you can help it.

No, it's not natural.

On New Year's Day, let's celebrate a fresh young year by deepening our silence and toughening our watch. Let's pause when we see reactions are guiding us rather than Silence. And let's pause again when we notice we are accepting an appearance of separation without asking Within for a second opinion.

Celebrate with me on the New Year! Let's eat, drink, and be merry ... and start our year off with a long, heady sip of God.

THE ARGUMENT

It happened one day that three Bikkhus were taking a walk in the morning sun. As they strolled along, chatting amiably, they passed by a pennant blowing in the wind. The first Bikkhu paused and said, "Look at that—the wind is in motion."

"No, no, no," said the second Bikkhu. "As any fool can tell, it is the pennant that is in motion."

"But you are entirely wrong," insisted the first Bikkhu, who was getting a little irate. "It is the wind that is moving. I can feel it."

"Nevertheless," replied the second Bikkhu, "all you need do is look, and you can tell that the motion comes from the pennant."

For several minutes the argument continued along these lines, with each man insisting he was right. Finally, the third Bikkhu, who had been silent all during this dialogue, spoke up.

"Dear friends! I am afraid you are both mistaken," he said, gently. 'What actually is moving is your own mind."

—Hui-neng

ANOTHER PING IN THE DREAM OF TIME

We need fresh starts.

It's so easy for our attention to slip out of God, out of Now, and back into our worn, old, tired way of looking. Fresh starts heal us of our slippages.

The morning, for example, is a daily fresh start—our chance to begin our day cloaked in peace. It's one of the most important moments of the day, because it sets our tone, directs our footsteps. Morning meditations can be miraculous, if we let them be.

And of course, any moment at all when we stop what we're doing, get still, and sink deep into God is a fresh start, pulling us gently away from too much gazing at the world. It leads us beside still waters.

Even the world likes new beginnings. Which is why everyone gets so excited at New Year's—it's seen as a clean fresh start, a chance to begin anew and possibly dash off into a bigger, brighter future. At least that's what beings everywhere hope will happen at New Year's.

But of course, it doesn't. Why? Because the human concept of starting fresh is to improve the ego, the human self. Think about it. How can a separated self ever improve? It can't. Oh, yes, it can dress itself up differently, but if you look closely, you'll see it's the same old faux self under the new costume. Separation by any other name is still separation. Only awareness of our Identity can dissolve the pull of the ego. Only when we begin to see that this sad little self is a delusion, does it begin to fade. Awareness heals. All other changes are cosmetic.

So I don't have to tell you that New Year's is not the time to sigh over the past, catalog our mistakes, and make long, useless lists of planned improvements. This is not a fresh start; this is trying to fix the dream. You already know this. You've tried it.

However, a period of silent meditation at New Year's is a whole other matter. This is an authentic step, because it invites our True Self to come forward. Silent listening can open our heart, open our eyes, open our ears, open our life.

Let's do it. Join with me at New Year's in Silence—you from wherever you are and I from wherever I am. In our Silence, we will unite in stepping back from the dream. And feel our severalness melt into One Pure Heart.

I salute your Hidden Splendor.

A TALE OF TWO CATERPILLARS

Maybe you've heard this delightful story before. It is attributed to Rev. Peter Marshall, a minister who was renowned for his creative story-telling.

It seems that two caterpillars, old friends, were soon about to dissolve into cocoons. Not surprisingly, the two of them fell to discussing this major journey into the unknown as they took their last slow crawl around the block together.

"It's over," said the first caterpillar mournfully. "We're done for. As all realists know, this life is all there is. When the cocoon thing happens, we lose everything: life, earth, grass, movement. Mark my words—when it happens, we're dead ducks."

"Hmmm," murmured the second caterpillar. "You know, it looks like that at first glance ... but still, something tells me you're wrong about it."

"How could I possibly be wrong?" said the other caterpillar crossly. "Any sensible creature knows that endings are endings, and that's that."

"Yes, but still ... I've got a funny feeling we'll end up soaring high in the blue sky, free as birds, bungee-jumping off clouds and skydiving head-first into a field of purple cornflowers."

"What a romantic," scoffed his buddy. "But honestly, I think you'd better face the facts. Reality is reality, my friend. Our time is up, and when you're done, you're done." And he glanced sadly over at the crisp green grasslets and the soft, dusty earth that had been his home.

"You're a good fellow, but all I can say is I'm positive you're mistaken about this," replied the other caterpillar.

"I'll tell you what you are," said his friend, looking annoyed. "You're a space cadet, that's what."

So that's how the two caterpillars spent their last, long day together. One certain it was all over, and the other knowing it was all just beginning.

And one of them was right.

THE ONE IS ALWAYS THE ONE

Here in our ever-shifting Good vs. Bad Universe, the world appears to be threatening itself with war again. Which means that now is a time when our highest consciousness of peace is called for.

There is no conflict within the One. No separate wills, no opposing beliefs, no divisions, no walls, no conflagrations, no factions, no greed, no insanity, no cruelty, no Prince of Darkness. The One is at-one. So our work in this kind of situation is simply asking to *see* the One Christ in everyone concerned. In other words, this crisis is a call to pray for the enemy.

As we begin to release our fear of terrorists and tyrants, there opens up a space in which we can sense the Love from which we all arise and in which we all dwell without end. The interesting thing about this sort of prayer is that it does not (and will not) appeal to our "common sense," which is always grounded in the belief in good and evil. Praying to see the Christ in aggressors is utter nonsense to the human mind. It is only the Divine One within us that understands the sanity of such a prayer. And it is He who reponds to our call with healing.

❧ ❧

From the notes of R.M. Bucke, a mystic who has written books about Walt Whitman and is the author of *Cosmic Consciousness:*

I saw that the universe is not composed of dead matter, but is, on the contrary, a living Presence; I became conscious in myself of eternal life. It was not a conviction that I would have eternal life, but a consciousness that I possessed eternal life then; I saw that all men are immortal; that the cosmic order is such that, without any peradventure, all things work together for the good of each and all; that the foundation principle of the world, of all the worlds, is what we call love, and that the happiness of each and all is in the long run absolutely certain. The vision lasted a few seconds and was gone, but the memory of it and the sense of the reality of what it taught has remained during the quarter of a century which has since elapsed.

— R.M. Bucke

MY MIRACULOUS MOVING CHURCH

When I first moved to San Francisco eight years ago, I found myself commuting to work via bus. It was a 30-minute ride, and the experience was new to me. In the beginning, faced with this longish stretch of empty time, I brought along books to keep myself entertained.

Yet a few days later, it came to me that this little bus ride provided me with a unique opportunity. There I was, 30 minutes with nothing to do and nowhere to go—why not meditate? So I began my private bus meditation program—got on board, sat down, closed my eyes, and sank into God.

At first it seemed a little unnatural. Voices and street noises inserted themselves into my silence like balloons piercing the sky. But as the days passed, a blessed inner Presence took over, and presently the noises subdued themselves into a harmless murmur. And so for the next three years I continued this comforting, silent practice every morning, every evening, week after week after week.

And then after some months, I noticed a subtle shift occuring in my busride. What happened was that the very moment I got on the bus, peace would settle upon me at once. Where before I had sought out peace, now it seemed peace rushed to greet me the instant I boarded my moving church.

And there was one other gift in store for me. After three years or so, I moved out of the city and no longer had occasion to travel by bus. But I would come back into the city and once again seek transport from the wonderful San Francisco Muni system. To my surprise, even after years of being away from my old habit of meditating on the bus, I found that that same luminous peace came to me—still!—the minute I sat down in a bus, anywhere.

It was as though the bus had become like one of those old brass candlesticks which, after months and years of burnishing, ends up with a richer, deeper glow than it had enjoyed when it was brand new.

And so my bus had become permanently burnished. To this day, for me, busses will forevermore travel much, much further than from one human location to another. Thanks to His grace, they carry me instantly, timelessly into God.

DEALING WITH GRIEF

Life is dotted with tragedies.

The question is, what do we do when one comes near us; the kind that rips us apart and sends us reeling? One of my own darkest moments was the sudden death of a close friend who was loved by many and who was, by all accounts, completely undeserving of so early a passage. Yet, there he was, and then—there he wasn't.

His name was Pete. The name suited him; it sounds friendly, down-to-earth, unswayed by trivia. And so was he. Like all others who knew Pete, I was devastated when he retired from planet earth and moved on. He had been friend, counselor, nurturer, mentor and humorist to many for several good years. His spirit was the sort that put spring into our days, good ones and bad ones, and his wisdom kept us on balance whenever we were in serious danger of veering off course.

So the day Pete left was an awful day for all of us who treasured him. A black day, full of grief and personal angst. How to reconfigure days and weeks without this incredible life force in it? In the beginning, at the first glimpse of a vanished friend, it does not seem possible. That's why we weep. Not for our friend, but for the sudden desperate vacuum in our own lives. At least it seems like a desperate vacuum.

As for Pete, we all knew he was managing; he was certainly in heaven, probably regaling angels with heaven and hell jokes and telling them what a fine job they were doing with reprobates like himself. Making them feel important; that was one of the things he did best.

And when he wasn't around to do that for me anymore, I took it hard. I remember feeling stunned, angry, baffled, bereft, heartbroken all at once. There's nothing unusual in that. Every being has these feelings around a death, and while we all know they eventually recede, that is a future fact, and it doesn't impact the awfulness of fresh grief in the slightest. I had one tool, though, that many of my friends did not. I knew about meditation.

Meditation—getting utterly silent and still— can make a difference to anything. I mean anything. I knew that, and shortly after I came face to face with my hot slice of sorrow over Pete, I did call on this tool. I sat down in my apartment, closed my eyes and lowered myself into the Silence. The first day it was only for a few moments. By the third day, I was able to do it for ten minutes. I wasn't asking for anything, or even waiting to hear anything—I was frankly just looking for some small connection with Peace.

After the meditation, my mind would jump fairly quickly back to feeling sad and bereft. So in the first few days, it certainly looked like getting silent was pointless.

I kept on with it, though, even though the large part of my day was soggy from moping. I kept on with it, simply because I had no other remedy for grief.

And here's what happened. At the end of the week, without warning, I woke up sharply in the middle of the night. I was wide awake, but unmoving, staring out of my uncovered windows. Since I lived high up in a multi-storied building, the view was a broad cityscape under an even broader sky. There I was, eyes wide, mouth open, frozen as a stone.

I was staring, because dead center in front of me was a full, bright, unwinking moon, so alive and so close it almost seemed touchable. All I know is the moon was shining full heat right on my face, and as it did, I understood that Pete was fine, and Pete was there.

"Hello, Pete," I said, and in that same moment, buckets of grief lifted away from me, leaving me as light-hearted as a child on the first day of summer vacation. Rivers of warmth washed over me.

I took one last fond look at that uniquely brilliant moon and then turned over and fell sound asleep.

STUCK SPOTS

Car horns are blazing loud. Traffic is stacked, and my friend is visibly upset.

I know that, because I'm riding alongside him, watching the rage creep upwards and overtake his face, voice, eyes, muscles, nerve endings. Even his clothes show their irritation—hot wrinkles are forming along the sleeves and neck of his shirt.

He wants to proceed, and the traffic is stuck, stopped, unmoving. It's more than he, a mover and doer, can bear; he has by now lost all sense of self and is simply a unit of frustration, searching wildly for an outlet. If he could heave the steering wheel into the mass of cars pinning him to one spot, he would. It's safely attached, however, so the issue doesn't come up.

My mood, on the other hand, is untroubled. But I take no credit for that—it's the way I'm wired. Standing still in a line of traffic doesn't happen to bother me, even if I'm late. Still, I know perfectly well what he's going through—I have other buttons equally charged. Buttons that wouldn't even flutter your eyelash can send me headlong into high-level irritation. Push them and I'm lost. So I'm no better; it's just that I'm missing the more popular traffic button. Lucky for him, because at that moment in time I was able to sit still, breathe deep, and spray a little quiet on his wave of angst.

Of course, eventually we escaped the stuck place and ended up cruising along without worry. My friend said, "I hate it when I get that upset," and I said, "Yes, me too—it's a prison." And he indicated he would like to liberate himself. At that I chuckled and said we all would. Escaping our mind-prisons is a lifelong adventure; all of us want to be free of sore spots. Some of us even want it enough to do something about it. And then we reviewed some of the ancient and time-honored methods for neutralizing reactive buttons. There are several techniques for deactivating explosive impulses; all of them involve jumping onto a different train of thought, one that is headed into pacific territory. And then staying on it.

An obvious first step, of course, is to notice you are overheating. At this point you are still captain of your ship and in a position to choose a cool-down. You remember you are a good and decent person and that inflammation nearly always leads to regret. You remind yourself that your spirit is way, way larger than any moment of crisis.

As a practical step, you can take a breath and count to ten, for instance. Or close your eyes and visualize a cool moving mountain stream, thickly bordered by trees. You can recall the face of a loved one, think about a well-cherished food, think about a favorite sport, think about anything at all except whatever is setting your gut on fire.

It helps to lose yourself in the new pictures. If you have chosen a sport to distract yourself away from hell, do a job of it. Revisit the most exciting game you ever saw; dwell on the moments of victory; rerun the plays that made the game famous; picture the faces of your heroes. If, for example, you are sitting in traffic, suffocated by immobility, run the game you love across your mind until it has won your full attention.

By the time you have finished with the game, your gut will be returned to a more normal state, and quite possibly the traffic flow will be breathing again. In any event, the five-alarm excitation you were entertaining will have paled and shrunk. As for you, you find yourself plucked out of hell and seated in grace—*you win.*

JUST KEEP WORKING ON YOU

There are many wonderful stories about Ramana Maharshi, the famous Indian teacher who experienced enlightenment at the surprising age of sixteen. This story is one of my favorites:

Apparently a student went to see Ramana Maharshi one day and said, "Sir, I am working very hard to discover my Real Self. Each day, just as you asked, I inquire, "Who Am I?" I meditate on the nature of God without fail. But there is one thing, sir, that keeps bothering me."

"And what is that?" asked the sage.

"Well," said the student, "I'm worried about the rest of the world. It's clear that we need many, many enlightened minds before this world is a happy place. My question for you now is: what can one do to assist other beings in waking up?"

Maharshi started laughing.

"Why do you worry yourself about other people?" he replied. "At night, a man falls asleep and has a dream that he is taking a walk in the country with a group of companions. In the morning when he awakes, he says, "Oh, it was just a dream!" and goes on about his business. At no time does he look around his room and say, "Oh, dear, I wonder if my dream companions are also awake?"

A Realization of the One Self

This is an ancient story about two young men who each longed to be accepted into the local Zen monastery.

One day the two approached the head priest of the monastery and asked what they might do to become accepted as students.

The head priest said, "First, I want both of you to find a chicken and take it deep into the forest, all alone. Then I want you to kill the chicken—but only when you are in a place where no one can observe you doing it."

The young men accepted their assignment and went on their way. The first found a chicken almost at once, entered into a remote section of forest and promptly killed it.

The second young man also found a chicken and, carrying it carefully in his hands, entered deep into the forest. He walked for miles and miles and miles.

"Alas, sir, I can't join the monastery. I failed your test," sighed the young man.

"How so?" asked the priest.

"I found a chicken quickly enough and went deep into the forest. I traveled for miles to be sure no one could see me when I killed it. But in the end, I saw that no matter how far I traveled, I could never find a place where my action would not be overseen."

"And why is that?" asked the high priest.

"Because no matter how remote the area I went to," said the young man. " there was always one present to observe my action. There was no way to escape this witness—because it was I who was the witness."

"Welcome to our monastery," said the high priest.

MEDITATIONS TO HELP YOU
THROUGH THE ROUGH SPOTS

Problems occur because we think we are small and separate and perishable, and from this dark perspective all manner of threats seem to loom at every corner. But in fact, we are greatly mistaken about being small and perishable. In Truth we are all born of God and are inseparable from His love.

Look without fear into the moment before you, and sooner or later you will encounter His light. Not only are you connected now and forever with this Light, but in fact it *is* your Real Self.

Recalling that Light deep within our soul is the purpose of everything that happens. And remembering we *are* the Light is why we're here.

The following poems have all come from divine inspiration, to assist you in rising above any concerns or rough spots in your life.

Self

hello
to your deep
luminous
beautiful Self
which is seen
without eyes

Selflessness

the reason
a bird sings
with such joy
is that
it does not
trouble itself
with a demand
for recognition

Decisions

the right
decision
is only heard
with a quiet mind

Courage

in this world
it takes courage
to remember
your Beauty

Insight

honor
the whispers
from your
heart

Belief

cure yourself
of yesterday's
beliefs
and you
are free
forever

Future

tomorrow
is yesterday
in different clothes,
unless you choose
to alter your fabric
today

Perfection

if you are
feeling insulted,
it is only because
you have forgotten
you are
perfect

Laughter

laughter
is heaven's
favorite
antibiotic

Beauty

only after
the butterfly
has discarded
its caterpillar shell
does it reveal
itself as
exquisite

Change

fear
no change
in either your body
or the earth,
for neither suffering
nor success
can ever touch
your Holy Self

Prison

every
grudge
you hold
is a
prison

God

That Which Never Dies
created us
That Which Never Dies
knows no fear
That Which Never Dies
cherishes us
That Which Never Dies
is right here

Complaints

angels
chuckle
over all your
complaints

Struggle

struggle
is necessary
until you discover
how to be
delighted
doing laundry

Violence

one of our
most common
delusions
is the belief
that we can violate
another
without hurting
ourself

Mirror

everything
you see
is simply
an image
of yourself:
bless it

Value

like your Self,
nothing
of true value
can ever
be lost

Kindness

every
single being
to whom you
are kind
returns you
a living waterfall
of silent blessing

Anger

anger
is just another
narcotic,
attractive to those
who have not yet
fallen in love
with Peace

Fear

fear
is a lie
about Who
You are

Infinity

God
is utterly
everywhere,
which is why
we don't
notice Him

Innocence

in
the eyes
of God,
you are as
innocent
as flowers

Forgiveness

forgiveness
is the holiest
of all actions,
for it mirrors
the thought
of the
Divine

Joy

even
a feather
can teach us
to rejoice
if we are willing
to learn joy

Cost

the price
you pay
for peace
is a heavy one:
you must release
all desire
for madness

Happiness

eat some
fresh happiness
for lunch

Purity

cleanse off
your mind
with Silence,
and heaven
will pour its music
into your heart

Esteem

regard
yourself kindly
in all you do,
for the greatest
miracle
on earth
is You

Choice

a master is one
who has learned how
to make a smile
instead
of a fist

Goodness

the only way
to learn about
your own goodness
is to discover it
in the face of
an enemy

Giving

be like a flower
standing tall,
freely offering
scent to all

Debt

debt is simply
a visible form
of hidden hurt;
release the hurt
and the debt will
disappear

Strength

you will never
be strong
as long as you think
you are the One
Who carries
your burden

Relationships

find the flower
in your partner's heart
and water it with
tender art;
Should the flower
choose not to stay,
let go!
Another
will come your way

Pain

when you feel pain,
treat yourself
gently,
the way you
treat a child
who sees a ghost

Partnership

you can
travel in joy
forever
once you find
the one
in whom you see
your own beauty

The Source

your song
is too rich
to come
from anywhere
but God

Order

hidden
beneath
all chaos
is a field of
bliss

Service

you are the hand
Love uses
to create Its
works of heart

Gratitude

thankfulness
is the lifeblood
of success

Death

a flower
falls back to the earth
from whence it
got its start,
yet the memory
of its radiance
burns forever
in our heart

Purpose

you are
already doing
what you are meant to do;
what you long for
is the thing
you are meant to do
tomorrow

Gentleness

gentleness
is the highest
expression of
strength

Friendship

a true friend
is one
who notices
your shadows
but chooses
to have faith
in your Light

Healing

end your friendship
with sadness
and healing arises
like cool
spring grass

Teacher

hear the water
running,
glistening:
telling secrets
if you're
listening

Judgment

when you cease
putting stones
in another's path,
your own way
opens up
like magic

Excellence

at every moment
the perfect movement
is poised within,
waiting for you
to say,
GO

Compassion

to look with
deep compassion
on our feelings,
good or bad,
is the first step
towards awakening

Endings

sometimes
the deepest way
to love
another person
and yourself
is to walk away

Insight

only the heart
that is open
and free of doubt
can set heaven
on fire

Illusions

a snake arose
from I know not where;
yet in the Silence
it wasn't there

Yielding

see how
the grass
in perfect ease
forgives with a bow
each thrusting
breeze

Awakening

stung by a tart lemon,
the tongue awakes;
struck by a whiff of God,
the mind opens

Here

here
is a huge
Place;
almost as vast
as You

Cleansing

empty of self,
empty of doubt:
only then
can our Radiance
start pouring out

Release

freedom
reveals itself
as soon as
you kiss
all your suffering
goodbye

Wealth

richer than gold;
wider than skies;
stronger than trees;
softer than sighs;
purer than music;
empty of sin:
this is the
Wealth
that awaits us
within

Emptiness

behold the miracle
of the vase:
its inner gift of
empty space

Communication

every tree,
every stone,
every whisper of wind
is answering
all your questions

Love

the sun shines
on a flower
for no reason
except love

Gift

the most
precious gift
you will ever open
is your heart

Sight

if you are
not seeing
Light
you are
not Seeing
at all

Unity

flower
or starling,
ant or elf:
every creature
is your Self

Meditation

simple stone
upon a hill,
teaching the art
of being still

Awareness

only after
you have
surrendered
your ego
does Seeing
begin

A SALUTE TO EVERYONE

There are thousands of us. We come from everywhere, have myriad histories, and belong to all kinds of singular denominations. As individuals, we're as ordinary as blades of grass—except for one detail. One way or another, we've found our feet firmly planted on a spiritual path, using this discipline or that, for the express purpose of reconnecting with our Real Self. We are sleeping angels, determined to wake up. Because waking up, we all know, is the path to happiness.

And yet, one of the first discoveries we make about this path is that it's not easy.

Life presents everyone with trials. But trials can seem even harder when you are attempting to view them in a new way, through the eyes of compassion. For those of us who are attempting to look at the world and our life without judgment, to break outside of the normal paradigms, it is no longer possible to just have a bad day. We have a bad day and then have it all over again because we feel guilty about allowing it to happen. Who knew stepping forward spiritually could be such a pain in the neck?

These letters are a hug and a high five to everyone who is putting authentic effort and true grit into awakening, because despite the inevitable pitfalls and potholes and "slippery when wet" moments, this work you are doing day by day by day is quite simply the most important work on earth.

—*Elsa Joy Bailey*

ABOUT THE AUTHOR

Elsa Joy Bailey began having mystical experiences at a very early age; in fact, she began receiving small poems when she was three. Not surprisingly, she did not grasp the inner truths within these poems until years later, when her mind had opened to Spirit.

During her adult years, Elsa 's love of writing led her into a career as an advertising copywriter. Yet all the while, she maintained an inexplicable interest in nonduality. Her curiosity led her into the works of Joel Goldsmith, *A Course in Miracles*, Rumi, Nisargadatta, Hafiz, Meister Eckhart, Hildegard of Bingen, Brother Lawrence, Evelyn Underhill, Jean Klein, Krishnamurti, and many, many others. To her, this community of conscious souls was living food.

In 1985, following a mind-shivering out-of-body experience, she became a committed seeker. This near-death experience arose from a serious respiratory illness. During the out-of-body period she was shown truths that had previously been revealed primarily through her reading. Now they were revealed as undeniable convictions.

After this event, she returned to the material realm completely healed and infused with a spiritual mission to share that which had been revealed. As many who have had similar experiences can attest, new unfoldments continued once the awakening had occurred.

Memos for Mystics is comprised of Elsa Joy's musings on the many "openings" one encounters on the spiritual path, as well as the inevitable pitfalls, backslides and sudden joys.

Made in the USA
Charleston, SC
29 July 2015